DATE DUE

NOV 17 2008	
JUL 2 0 2009	

BRODART, CO.   Cat. No. 23-221-003

choosing and
raising a cat

choosing and raising a cat

Caroline Davis and Elizabeth Perry

BARNES & NOBLE

NEW YORK

This edition published by Barnes & Noble Publishing, Inc.,
by arrangement with Hamlyn, an imprint of Octopus Publishing
Group Limited

2005 Barnes & Noble Books

M 10 9 8 7 6 5 4 3 2 1

ISBN 0-7607-7479-X

Copyright © Octopus Publishing Group Ltd 2005

A CIP catalogue record for this book
is available from the British Library

Printed and bound in China

CONTENTS

Introduction

What could be better than relaxing on the sofa with a soft, purring cat on your lap, or returning from a hard day's work to be greeted by your feline friend miaowing joyfully at your return? A creature of opposites, a cat is independent yet loves companionship, is gentle yet a skilful hunter, loves to play yet sleeps for most of the day. He has a mind of his own and you always know what he wants. If you have ever owned a cat, you will know what an empty place a house is without one. If you have never owned a cat, once you have one in your home you will soon realize that there was something missing before.

You may have decided that a cat is the right pet for you, but will you be the right owner for a cat? Can you afford the expense of caring for an animal that may live for 20 years or more? Are you prepared to consider your cat when you move house, start a family or change jobs? Will you ensure he has the space he needs, the right food and necessary health care? If the answer to all these questions is 'yes', then you can take the next step to becoming a cat owner.

This book will show you how to choose a cat that will fit in well with your lifestyle, where to get him, how to make sure he is healthy, how to understand about his needs in the home and what to expect once he is settled. With this knowledge, you can be sure that your cat will be happy with you and that you will be the perfect cat owner.

It can be very confusing trying to decide which colour cat you want, but there's far more to choosing your ideal pet than simply opting for black or white. There are lots of breeds, ranging from the hairless Sphynx to the Kurilian Bobtail, all with different personalities. Find out all you need to know from the breed section to help you choose the cat of your dreams.

Note

In this book, the terms 'he', 'him' and 'his' are used to refer to all cats, whether male or female.

A contented cat means a contented owner. Together you'll have many years of companionship and fun.

INITIAL QUESTIONS

You have decided that you want a cat as a pet, but have you stopped to consider whether you will be giving him the ideal home – one that provides him with everything he needs for a contented and long life? You should consider carefully all aspects of being a cat owner before you take on such a long-term commitment.

Why do you want a cat?

The first thing to consider is why you want a cat. Do you love animals and caring for them? Is it for companionship or a pet for the children? Do you want to breed pedigree cats or perhaps show your cat? Be sure that you have spent time considering why you want a cat. It is all too easy to fall in love with a cute kitten in the pet shop, then, before you know it, you have committed yourself to caring for him for the next two decades.

If you are single, then you need to consider only what you want; but in a family home all members of the family should be consulted. An animal needs to feel safe and secure in his home and will be aware of any hostility from any member of the family. Make sure everyone understands that a cat is a long-term commitment, and that he should be treated with respect and love.

Cats and children

It is a widely held misconception that a cat may jump into a cot or pram and accidentally smother a baby while he is sleeping. This is highly unlikely to happen, but if you have a baby and are concerned then buy a 'cat net', which covers the cot or pram and prevents the cat from jumping into it. It is also a good idea to shut the cat out of the nursery.

It is not a good idea to get a cat if you have young children, unless you are prepared to keep a close eye on any interaction. Toddlers can unintentionally intimidate and hurt a cat and, likewise, the cat will defend himself against unwanted attention from a child and may scratch and bite.

Can you afford a cat?

A cat will need good-quality food to stay healthy.

You should take into consideration food, vaccinations, veterinary bills, cattery fees, insurance, toys, litter and bedding. A cat is a long-term investment, so you need to be sure you will be able to meet the cost of caring for your cat for the next 20 years, or even longer.

Where you get your kitten or cat from will determine how much he is going to cost (see page 26). Added to this is the cost of the equipment you will need (see pages 130–133). If you get an older cat, he should already have been neutered, whereas a kitten will require vaccinations and neutering within the first few months. All cats need worming and defleaing on a regular basis as well as annual booster vaccinations (ask a vet how much this is likely to cost); and even healthy cats will need veterinary care as they get older.

It is a good idea to insure your cat in case of accident, illness or, in the case of pedigree cats, theft. There are many different types of insurance, so choose carefully.

Initial questions

Providing the ideal home

Warmth, food and love are essential to a cat's well-being, as is the ability to exercise in a safe environment. He will need a cosy bed, toys, healthy food, a scratch post, a litter tray and veterinary care. If you are going to keep your cat indoors, he will also need an activity centre so that he can jump and stretch, as well as daily play sessions with you to keep him fit and healthy.

Is your home suitable?

You must be able to provide a suitable environment for your cat. If you are planning to allow your cat to go outside, then a quiet cul-de-sac, away from busy roads, is ideal. Note that many rescue centres will not rehome a cat to people who live near busy roads, and breeders will also want to know what kind of environment you are taking a kitten into. Remember that this is for the sake of the animal to ensure he goes to a safe home.

Don't despair if this applies to you, because there are other options. You can enclose your garden so that your cat can't escape, or build a run so that he has access to

fresh air but is perfectly safe from danger. Alternatively, you can keep your cat indoors, as long as you are prepared to provide him with the stimulation he will need. Some older cats, or cats with disabilities, are perfectly content to live indoors, while many people choose to keep their cat inside to prevent them being injured or stolen, or getting lost.

Think about whether you are prepared to provide your cat with the space he needs. If you were to keep him indoors, would you be happy allowing him to wander freely around the entire house? Could you devote an entire room to your cat, turning it into a 'cat room' kitted out with everything he needs to exercise? Note that, in terms of territory, a three-bedroom house can accommodate only two indoor cats.

Other pets

Cats can get along very well with other pets, especially if introduced as kittens. However, will your current pets be happy with a stranger in their midst? Small animals, such as mice and hamsters, are natural prey to a cat and should be kept in a secure place to which the cat does not have access. If introduced properly, cats and dogs can live in harmony, and even become close friends. Some dogs, though, may never be happy with a feline in the house and the cat may have to be returned.

Left: A garden will provide plenty of room for your cat to explore and exercise.

Right: Cats need to be stimulated to avoid boredom and behavioural problems.

Living with a cat

It is true that cats are independent animals and will
spend hours sleeping or hunting and exploring outside,
but they still like a routine and can judge almost to the
minute their mealtimes. If you spend a lot of time at
work or away on holiday, your cat won't get the
attention and love he deserves.

Are you a house-proud person who likes everything to
be clean and gleaming? If so, you should consider
whether a cat is a suitable pet. Although cats moult
primarily during the spring and summer, central heating
means that cats now shed hair all year round. Hair on
furniture and carpets is inevitable, and clothes too are a
magnet for hair. In wet weather, you may find muddy
pawprints leading from the cat flap through the house.

Another consideration is damage. Kittens love climbing
curtains and chewing fabric, while older cats strop their
claws on the edges of sofas and armchairs. In addition,
cats can and do have 'accidents', particularly if they
are unwell and unable to reach their litter tray in time;
vomit, hairballs and dead prey must also be cleaned up.

Planning for the long term

Before deciding whether or not to get a cat, it is worth
considering what plans you have for the future. Cats
can live for many years and in that time your
circumstances may change.

Kittens love climbing, and even though their
claws are tiny, they can do significant
damage to curtains.

Consider whether you are a house-proud person who would
not be happy with hair on the furniture and carpets, or
whether you would appreciate the 'help' of a feline friend.

Consider the following:
- Do you rent your property?
- Are you allowed pets?
- Do you travel a lot?
- Are you planning to have children?
- Do you spend a lot of time at work/out socializing?

Because cats can live for many years, you should think
about the future and consider what will happen to the
cat if you are no longer able to care for him. Do you
have a family or friends who would be happy to give
him a home? Older owners in particular should give this
consideration. Making arrangements in advance will
give you peace of mind.

Adult or kitten?

You know you want a cat, but now you have to decide if you want an adult cat or a kitten. If it is your first cat, you may love the idea of owning a cute, fluffy kitten and be happy to take on the responsibility of owning a young cat. Alternatively, you may have decided to offer a home to an older cat. Both adults and kittens have advantages and disadvantages to consider.

Adult cats

In many ways an adult cat is much easier to care for than a kitten. An adult cat is already litter-trained and will use his litter tray immediately. He is not as inquisitive and is more able to take care of himself, so is less likely to have accidents. An adult cat is usually neutered and vaccinated and, if well socialized, happy around people.

Adult cats can, however, be an unknown quantity, particularly if they are from a rescue centre where they have been taken in as a stray. They will have no medical

An adult cat is easier to care for than a kitten.

history and may carry viruses or other diseases. They may have learned to be fearful of humans if they have previously been neglected or badly treated, and this can lead to behavioural problems. It is also harder to integrate an adult cat with resident pets of any type, so the settling-in period may take longer, which can be stressful for both parties.

Advantages
- No toilet training required
- More able to care for himself
- More streetwise
- Less likely to have accidents
- Already neutered
- Character of the cat is already known
- More sociable

Disadvantages
- May have behavioural problems
- Unknown health history (fear of infectious diseases – see page 33)
- Cannot be kept as an indoor cat if previously allowed out of the house
- Less adaptable with other pets
- Limited lifespan

Kittens are such fun to play with, but they need to have careful supervision to prevent accidents.

Kittens

Tiny kittens are a joy to watch as they explore their new home; they love playing but also sleep for long periods. Yet a kitten is a big responsibility and needs careful supervision. His inquisitiveness can lead him into trouble, as he can squeeze into the tiniest gaps, such as behind gas fires. A kitten is not as quick at getting out of the way of closing doors and people's feet, and is less able to defend himself against the rough handling of young children.

A kitten will have frequent toilet accidents and requires several meals during the day. Unless well socialized in a family environment from birth, he will be frightened when first taken to his new home and is likely to hide for long periods of time.

However, a kitten can be integrated far more easily than an adult cat, and will quickly learn his pecking order with other cats or pets in the house. You will have the joy of seeing him grow and develop, and know that he should have a long life ahead of him. If you get two kittens together, particularly if they are siblings, they will quickly learn to get along. However, bear in mind that sociability is dependent on their personality.

Advantages
- More adaptable
- Easier to train
- Long lifespan
- Knowledge of health history
- Easier to integrate with existing pets

Disadvantages
- Needs to be litter-trained
- More likely to get into scrapes
- More timid initially
- More likely to damage furnishings
- Needs more supervision
- Needs frequent meals

Initial questions

Making the right decision

Consider the following questions before deciding whether to opt for a kitten or an adult cat.

Are you house-proud?

Are you prepared for 'accidents', which will need cleaning up? Kittens may be small but they have sharp claws that will damage furniture and fabrics as they explore their new home. Can you accept that your curtains and wallpaper may be damaged?

Do you have the time for a kitten?

Kittens cannot be left alone for long periods of time; they need feeding at regular intervals and more attention during the day. Adult cats are more independent.

Which is best for your other pets?

If you have a cat already, he will quickly teach a kitten his place. However, if you introduce another adult, you will need to be prepared for a period of integration that could involve fights.

If you have a dog, is it safe to leave him with a kitten?

Some breeds of dog may view a kitten more as prey than as a playmate. You could ask your vet for advice on this matter.

Are your children too young to handle a kitten?

You may want your children to have the experience of raising a young kitten, but very young children (under the age of 5) may not realize when they are hurting their new pet. Older cats will defend themselves and escape.

How quickly do you want a cat?

It is worth considering that there are far more adult cats available than kittens. You may have to wait some time for a kitten, particularly if you want a pedigree. Rescue centres, however, are always full of healthy, loving adult cats looking for a new home, and, once the appropriate checks have been made, you will be able to adopt one almost immediately.

You may dream of having a cat curled up on your lap, but consider your lifestyle before deciding to buy one. It's better to wait for the right time than cause unhappiness in the home.

An older cat can still provide you with many years of love and companionship but is less demanding than a kitten or young adult.

Older cats

If you have decided to have an adult cat, it is worth considering taking on an older adult. Very often these make ideal companion cats, often wanting nothing more than a warm lap to sleep on. The fact that he is older means that he will need a regular veterinary check-up. Although cats over the age of 8 are now considered to be on the point of entering old age, you should still have many years of companionship to enjoy with your cat.

Male or female?

If your cat is to be neutered, then, apart from the male being larger, there is little difference between male and female cats. Some people believe that neutered males are more loving than females, but it really depends on the personality of different cats and the way in which they have been raised.

One cat or two?

Cats are very companionable animals and, although they are by nature solitary creatures, most cats seek interaction with either a human or another animal at some time. However, this does not necessarily mean that all cats would welcome a second feline in their home. So, when deciding whether or not to adopt one or two cats, consider the following points.

One cat

Although cats generally live and hunt alone in the wild, feral cats will group together and female feral cats will nurse each other's offspring. If you are at home for most of the day, and can spend time playing and interacting with your cat, then he may well be content to live as a single feline. Alternatively, another pet, such as a dog that gets on well with the cat, can provide the companionship he needs. An introverted cat may be happier living on his own and will be unhappy if a second cat is introduced. If you already own a cat and he is happy and healthy, it may be better to refrain from purchasing another cat.

One cat will be happy if he has plenty of attention from his owner.

Owning two cats may be twice the work, but it can also be twice the fun.

Two cats

If you are out at work all day, a second cat will provide companionship for the first. They will play and may even sleep together. Cats brought up as siblings usually get on well together whether they are male, female or one of each. Cats introduced to each other when kittens quickly learn their pecking order and, although one may be more dominant, they will establish a hierarchy and co-exist quite comfortably. Two adult cats who have lived together previously are usually friends.

However, having two or more cats does present problems. Unless they know each other, cats can be extremely fussy about whom they choose as their friends. Introducing a second cat may cause behavioural problems as the resident cat seeks to assert his dominance over his territory. It may take weeks, months or even a year for them to bond; or they may simply call a truce from the start and curl up together. In the worst-case scenario, the cats start fighting and don't stop. If this happens, and you have given them time to settle in and get to know one another, you may eventually decide that they will never get on and one will have to be rehomed.

Owning two cats is more expensive and doubles the cost of food, litter and veterinary bills. Remember that each cat should have his own bed, litter tray and food bowls. It is also twice the work, with two litter trays to clean and twice as much hair to vacuum, and more damage is caused to curtains and furniture.

Tips on introducing a new cat

Proper introductions can mean the difference between two cats becoming the best of friends or ending up as permanent enemies (see pages 139–140).

- Don't immediately shut two cats in a room together – such a traumatic experience could prevent any chance of future bonding.
- Don't expect miracles. Like humans, cats need time to get to know one another and it may take some time for them to be comfortable co-existing in the same house.

- Always show the resident cat plenty of love and affection. If he has always slept on your bed, continue to allow him to do so, shutting the other cat out of the room. This reassures the cat that he is still loved and needed and has not been usurped by the newcomer.

Introducing a kitten to an older cat

A cat that is already established in the house will naturally consider it to be his territory, and so another cat encroaching on it can lead to animosity between the two. If a kitten is brought in as a companion cat, the adult may be quite violent, attacking and hissing at the

Careful introductions are essential for a new cat to bond with his new family.

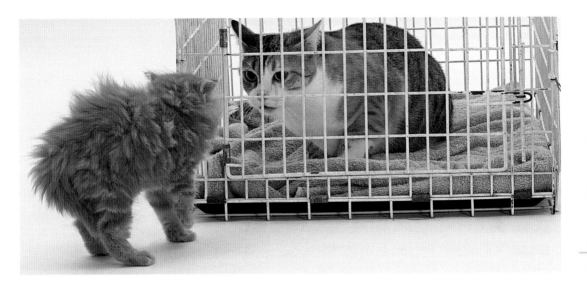

new animal. Introduce them carefully and separate them if they start to fight; kittens cannot defend themselves against a fully grown adult.

Buying or borrowing a cat pen can make introductions less stressful for both the new cat and resident pets.

Breed characteristics

Cats of all breeds may be sociable providing they are well socialized at a young age, though some breeds are more gregarious and do need the company of other cats for play and companionship. In particular, Siamese and the Oriental breeds may become depressed as the only pet in the house. If you want a pedigree cat, discuss with the breeder whether the cat would prefer a feline companion. If you are considering adopting two cats from different breeds, refer to the respective breeders to see if they are compatible.

Three or more cats

Behaviourists believe that an average three-bedroom house has enough space for only two cats to live together comfortably. Of course, many households have three, four or even more cats, which, while they may seem to be happy, does mean that their territory is severely restricted and can lead to behavioural problems. These may resolve over time as the cats bond. (See the behaviour problems section on page 166.)

What type of cat?

After deciding whether to get an adult or kitten, one cat or two, the time comes to decide whether to have a pedigree, non-pedigree or a cross-breed – a cat that is a combination of two pedigree breeds. Unless you have already chosen a particular breed, it is worth considering each option carefully.

Pedigree cats

Usually, pedigree cats are acquired directly from a breeder and the cat will come with documentation to prove he is a pedigree. Both parents of a pedigree cat must themselves be pedigrees. Although some pedigree cats may look similar, they can have widely differing temperaments. When you buy a pedigree kitten as a pet, you will usually be asked by the breeder to agree to neuter the kitten so that you cannot breed from him. To see a huge variety of pedigree cats, visit a cat show where breeders will be happy to talk about the characteristics of the cats they breed.

Advantages
- You can identify which breed best suits the lifestyle you can offer.
- You can choose one with a temperament you prefer.
- The cat's coat can be the colour and hair length you want.
- Pedigrees are sold as kittens.
- It is easy to obtain siblings if you want two kittens.
- The medical history and temperament of the parents will be available.

Disadvantages
- Pedigree kittens are expensive.
- You may have to wait months before your choice of kitten is available.
- They are more prone to specific illnesses and are more sensitive to environmental and dietary changes.
- Because of the above, they are more expensive to care for in terms of veterinary bills and specialist food.
- Pedigree cats are more expensive to insure.
- Certain breeds are more prone to behavioural problems than others.

A pedigree cat offers exactly your choice of coat type and colour as well as personality.

Initial questions

There are lots of beautiful, loving non-pedigree cats who need a good home.

Non-pedigree cats

Both parents of a non-pedigree cat will also be non-pedigree and, although many people believe their cat looks exactly like a particular breed, without a documented history it is unlikely to be a pedigree. Non-pedigree cats are just as rewarding as pedigree cats and are widely available from a variety of sources.

Advantages

- Non-pedigree cats are easily available, particularly adult rescue cats.
- They are generally long-lived and don't have specific health problems.
- They are free or relatively inexpensive.
- There is a huge choice of types and coat colours.

Disadvantages

- The parental history and temperament is unknown.
- If you want a specific colour or type, you may have to wait or search for the one you want.
- If the cat is older, you will have no knowledge of how he has been treated previously, which may affect his behaviour.
- Kitten availability may be limited at certain times.

Cross-breeds

Cross-breeds are a mix of any two pedigree breeds. They can therefore combine characteristics of breeds you find particularly attractive, though you may have to wait or search to find the combination of the two breeds you want. Remember that, although you will know the parentage and history of the animal, the breeding of the two pedigrees may result in the worst characteristics of both being combined in the offspring. Research breeds carefully and ask the breeder for advice on your choice of cross-breed.

Choosing a pedigree cat breed

You may decide you want a pedigree cat and have a preference for a particular breed. However, for the sake of all concerned, it is important that you consider carefully whether that type of cat is the most appropriate for your circumstances. The breeds section (see pages 56–127) enables you to see which types of cat are available, and which will suit both your needs and theirs. The chart opposite provides at-a-glance advice on finding the right cat for a mutually rewarding relationship.

Consider carefully which breed is suitable for your lifestyle, so that you are both happy.

Visit the breeder to see the mother and kittens together.

Choosing a cross-breed

If you choose a cross-bred cat, it is essential that you research the character traits of each parent. For example, a Burmese–Siamese cross can be very demanding since both breeds are attention-seeking (and often highly strung), vocal and extremely active. If you want a really interactive, exotic, 'talkative' and entertaining pet, then this could be the ideal cross-breed for you. If you prefer a laid-back, cuddly and affectionate cross-breed, with a plush coat, that simply adores humans, then you should consider a British Blue–Ragdoll cross.

Remember, however, that although the characters of pedigrees are fairly standard, there can be exceptions to the rules – so the personality, temperament and characteristics you expect from a particular cross may not, in fact, materialize in the kitten you buy, which could be a big disappointment.

FINDING THE RIGHT BREED

Type of owner(s)

Short, easy-care coat

Semi-/long coat

Young working couple; high-rise flat with enclosed balcony; first-time cat owners; indoor, independent, characterful pet required

Siamese, Oriental Shorthair, Bombay, Sphynx, Egyptian Mau, Singapura, Ocicat and Rex cats

Balinese, Oriental Longhair (Angora), Turkish Angora and Tiffanie

---

Single person; town house, with small rear garden and cat pen for outside safety and security; experienced cat owner; soulmate, affectionate, 'talkative' cat required

Particularly suitable are the Oriental Shorthair, Bombay, Ocicat, Siamese and Burmese; less vocal are the Snowshoe, Russian Blue, Korat, Tonkinese, Singapura, Bombay, Japanese Bobtail, Manx and American Curl

Any of the semi-/longhairs except Somali and Maine Coon, as these breeds dislike being confined inside or in a pen. Particularly suitable are the Birman and Balinese; Ragdoll and Cymric are also good choices, but are generally not as vocal

---

Couple with young children and other pets (dog, rabbit, other cat); semi-rural house, large garden; experienced cat owners; sociable, easily integrated, kind, laid-back, affectionate, playful cat required

British Shorthair, American Shorthair, Chartreux, Snowshoe, Abyssinian, Russian Blue, Burmese, Tonkinese, Singapura, Manx and Selkirk Rex

Particularly suitable is the Birman; other suitable cats include the Persian, Chinchilla, Maine Coon, Norwegian Forest, Ocicat and Burmilla

---

Older couple; country house with stables and land; experienced cat owners; large, 'cuddly', affectionate pet/mouser required

Adult non-pedigree; cross-breed (with large, 'cuddly' parents); British Shorthair, American Shorthair, Exotic Shorthair, Burmilla, European Shorthair and Manx

Maine Coon, Persian (particularly Tabby, Red, Blue-Cream and Colourpoint), Chinchilla, Norwegian Forest and Siberian Forest

Initial questions

FINDING A CAT

Finding the right cat for you is the next step. There is a wide choice of places you can go to obtain a cat, particularly if you are looking for a non-pedigree. Always visit the breeder, rescue centre or owner to see the cat or kitten before committing yourself to making a purchase. Give yourself time to consider the options as well: you may regret an impulse buy.

Where to obtain a cat

Rescue centres

There are many different rescue centres (see 'Rehoming a rescue cat' on pages 28–33). Many of the more popular pedigree breeds now have their own rescue organizations, which rescue and rehome lost and unwanted pedigree cats. They will want to ensure that you have the right home for that particular breed and will charge a fee for the cat. Perhaps the most common of these are Persian rescue centres.

Pedigree breeders

See pages 34–35 for details.

Friends or family may want to find homes for kittens.

Kittens are still available from pet shops, but ensure they are clean and healthy before purchasing one.

and you won't be provided with clear details about the kittens' history or parentage.

Newspaper advertisements

Cats and kittens are often advertised in the classified section of local newspapers. Here you may also see adverts from local rescue centres that need homes for unwanted cats.

Family and friends

Ask family and friends if they know of anyone with kittens requiring a good home.

Stray cats

See page 33 for advice about taking in a stray cat.

Vets

Veterinary clinics often advertise stray or unwanted kittens, or cats looking for good homes, on notice boards in their waiting rooms.

Shops

Some pet shops still sell non-pedigree kittens. Always check that the premises are clean and the kittens are alert and healthy. Check that the litter tray has been emptied and the food bowls are clean. It's unlikely that the shop will tell you where they have bought the kittens

Holidays

It would be very unfair to leave a cat soon after you have brought him home, so wait until you have returned from holiday before getting a new cat. If you already have a cat and you have been away, wait a while before introducing a new cat, as your original pet will need to feel secure in his home again, particularly if he has been in a cattery.

Finding a cat

Rehoming a rescue cat

Worldwide there are many thousands of cats of all types and ages in rescue centres, with just as many being 'put down' on a weekly basis. Cats and kittens are in centres for many different reasons, but they all need a home with someone to care for and love them. So, before you rush out to buy an expensive pedigree kitten, consider giving an unwanted feline a good home.

Rescue centres

There are many different rescue centres across the world, some providing sanctuary for cats only, while others take in all sorts of pets. There are also many smaller, independent rescue groups, most of which are well run and where the cats are well cared for.

Beware the individual person who 'rescues' cats, with many animals kept on their premises. Although the person imagines they have the best intentions, the cats may not be receiving the individual care they require in order to be well socialized, and they may be traumatized by a lack of the space they need to establish a territory. Such cats may not be the easiest to acclimatize into a home environment.

If you are looking for a pedigree cat, contact breed clubs, as they usually have a 'rescue' arm. These cats may be looking for new homes through no fault of their own. For example, their owners may have developed an allergy, have relocated or died. You will normally be asked to make a donation to the rescue centre to help it cover the cost of feeding and caring for the cat while in their care.

Potential owners

In most cases, you cannot simply walk into a rescue centre and take home your chosen cat on the same day. Staff need to satisfy themselves that potential owners can offer a suitable home. For this reason, many organizations insist on meeting the whole family and paying a home visit to check out the facilities before deciding whether or not a person would offer the kind of home they approve of. Centre staff are looking for potential owners with a confident, caring approach. They will assess how you speak to and handle the cat and will expect you to show a keen interest in cat care.

Centre staff usually do their best to match a cat to the new owner. Having taken details of a person and their requirements, they will then see if there is a cat available that would suit them, and vice versa. Some centres do not rehome cats to people who:

- Are out at work all day
- Have young children
- Have a dog or other cats
- Live next to or near a busy road
- Want a cat to give as a gift

Spend some time with your chosen cat at the centre to ensure you take to each other, rather than discover that you don't when you get home.

Centres often find that 'gift cats' are unwelcome presents and are frequently returned. The centre's other criteria are because:

- The cat may not get as much attention as he needs, which often leads to behaviour problems.
- Young children tend to mishandle and torment pets unintentionally.
- Having too many animals can result in them not getting enough individual attention and care, as well as the territorial problems that can be encountered.
- There is a real risk of the cat being injured or killed.

Behaviour

Once you have chosen your potential pet, find out as much as you can about his background from the centre staff. Some cats, for example, may not be house-trained or socialized, particularly feral (semi-wild) cats, so they may not integrate well into a domestic environment. If a cat's age is not known, there are no reliable indicators for determining how old he is.

If a cat was abused by humans in the past, he may need a lot a patience, time and understanding before he learns to trust you, and taking on such a cat is not easy. However, as you develop a relationship with the cat you will reap rewards as he bonds with you and becomes a loving cat. The main one is in knowing that he has a safe and kind home with you. If behaviour problems do arise, then the centre from which you got the cat will be happy to advise you.

Cost

Rescue centres usually ask for a donation when you collect your cat from them. The amount depends on the centre: some charge a set fee which is non-negotiable, while others are happy to accept whatever you can afford so long as they are satisfied you can afford to keep a cat.

The fee covers the cost of neutering and vaccinating the cat, as well as contributing towards his care while there. However, this fee often does not cover the whole cost, especially if the cat has received veterinary attention. Cats are often microchipped before being rehomed, so bear this in mind when you are asked to pay for a rescue cat. Younger kittens may be too young to be neutered before they are rehomed so, in most cases, centres will ask you to sign a form confirming that you will take the kitten to be neutered once he is old enough. If you are on a low income, the charity may provide financial assistance towards the cost of the procedure.

In the majority of cases, the centre retains legal ownership of the cat for the duration of his life, and may visit from time to time to ensure the cat is being cared for appropriately; if they judge he is not, they can take him back.

Some rescue cats appear timid and anti-social in a rescue centre, but are simply intimidated by the atmosphere and close proximity to other cats, becoming affectionate companions once rehomed.

An older rescue cat can make the perfect pet. Like all older cats, he will enjoy plenty of companionable cuddles.

Elderly cats

If you decide to acquire a cat from a rescue centre, then as well as finding yourself a pet you will have the additional pleasure of knowing that you have probably saved a life – many unwanted animals are destroyed simply because no suitable home can be found for them. Elderly felines in particular are difficult to rehome, since many people prefer to choose younger cats as they usually live longer than their older counterparts, so the person is likely to be able to enjoy their pet for a good number of years. So if you want a quiet, laid-back pet then it is worth considering a mature cat. (For more information about caring for older cats, see pages 194–201).

Health

Rescue cats are normally passed fit enough to be rehomed beforehand, but do beware of taking on an animal that does not look 100 per cent sound, or one that (if they are aware of it) the centre admits is carrying a viral illness such as feline leukaemia (FeLV) or feline immunodeficiency virus (FIV) – although in many cases such cats are put to sleep to prevent the spread of these diseases. Some afflicted cats can look perfectly well but are carriers of these diseases, so other cats that come into contact with them are at risk. However, if the carriers are kept solely indoors, they can still lead long and happy lives, so if you can provide such a home then this is ideal.

Some rescue organizations offer a scheme whereby, after rehoming, older cats with conditions that need ongoing age-related medical treatment are treated free of charge, thereby reducing the financial burden to potential owners.

Strays

Stray cats sometimes find a new home by themselves. If you are feeding a stray and want to give him a permanent home, first make every effort to ensure that the cat does not already have an owner. Check to see if he is wearing a collar and if he is well fed and groomed. Some older cats may look like strays because their coat is dull and scruffy, but this does not mean that they don't have a good home elsewhere.

Remember that, just because the cat appears regularly to feed in your garden, it does not mean he is a stray. He may just be greedy and taking advantage of extra meals while his owners are at work. Ask your neighbours (up to a couple of streets in each direction) if they own a cat answering to his description.

If you are sure the cat is a stray, take him to your vet, where he can be scanned to check if he has a microchip. Alternatively, go to your nearest rescue centre, where staff will make every effort to find the cat's owners. If he is unclaimed, you may be able to adopt him as your pet.

Fostering

Older people who would like a cat but are worried they may predecease their pet might like to consider fostering one from a rescue centre for the short or long term.

In this situation, the carer has the pleasure of a cat to look after and cuddle, along with the back-up of the centre with regard to advice and help when needed, and also the reassurance that the cat will be taken back for rehoming if the carer cannot manage or the cat outlives them. It is worth contacting rescue centres in your area to see if they offer such a scheme.

Finding a cat

Pedigree breeders

If you have decided to opt for a pedigree cat, you will need to find a breeder with kittens available for sale. Some breeds are very popular, so there are many breeders of these cats. However, their popularity means that there is a high demand for them, so you may have to put your name on a waiting list; then it may be several months before you can have your kitten.

Finding a breeder

Remember that you may have to travel some distance in order to purchase the pedigree cat you want. Contact the relevant breed club of the pedigree breed you desire. They will be able to provide you with a list of breeders who will have kittens for sale.

You may need to call several breeders to find the breed of kitten you're looking for.

Once you have decided on the right breeder, you will need to find out when they will have kittens available. Remember, if you have set your heart on a specific sex or colour, you may be disappointed. Queens don't always produce on demand, and there may be other people ahead of you on the waiting list with the same requirements. Try to be flexible, or you may have to wait even longer; for some breeds, you may have to wait up to a year for your kitten.

You may be asked to pay a deposit to secure the kitten. Check that this is refundable if you change your mind. Also check that the breeder gives you the following documentation when you collect your kitten:

- Signed personal pedigree form with your kitten's registration numbers.
- Application for transfer of ownership – until this slip is completed and returned with a fee to the appropriate association you will not be the kitten's official owner.

Finding a cat

- Vaccination card. This should detail vaccinations for feline enteritis and cat flu, and may also include vaccinations against feline leukaemia and chlamydia.
- Diet sheet detailing how much and when your kitten should be fed.
- Insurance documents. Your kitten should be insured for at least the first few weeks. They should detail the kitten's value and contain the insurance cover note.
- A separate agreement form. Many breeders now ask owners to sign an agreement to neuter the kitten so that you cannot breed from him.

Cross-breeds and queens

Breeders sometimes also offer cross-breed cats, whether bred deliberately or as an accident. Contact breeders to see if they are likely to have the type of cat you want. Breeders will retire a queen after a number of years, and may offer her up for adoption after she has been spayed. This may be a cheaper way to get the pedigree you want.

Top tip

You will have to wait until your kitten has been weaned before you can collect him (usually at 13 weeks for a pedigree), though you should be allowed to visit him. If you are not happy with any aspect of the kitten, you are entitled to withdraw from the sale. See the section on choosing a healthy cat (pages 36–41).

Check that all your kitten's documentation is in order before leaving the breeder's home.

Choosing a healthy cat

You have made your decision about exactly what kind of cat would be able to live happily in your home. Before you set off to choose your ideal cat, first do some research so that you understand the needs of the cat and can make the right choice. Any preparation work that you do will pay off, as it will ensure that you buy the right cat at the right time from the right place.

Be absolutely sure

Before going ahead, take time once more to consider carefully your circumstances (see pages 8–25). It can be a difficult time for both of you, so here are the questions you should ask yourself again before buying a cat:

- Can you financially support a cat?
- Are you likely to be changing jobs or working longer hours in the near future?
- Are you planning to move house within the next few months?
- Are you planning to start a family soon, or is a baby already due?
- Do you have any holidays booked?
- Are you getting a cat because you are unhappy?
- Are you planning to have a big party or have you been invited to numerous parties?
- Are you about to have an operation?

You may think that a cat will help you through a difficult period in your life. However, as with all animals, cats are extremely sensitive to humans' moods, and you will transmit your anxiety to your new cat (anxiety transference), making it difficult for him to settle in.

Preparation

Do some research beforehand about the type of cat you are taking on, and be prepared with a list of questions that you want to ask. A reputable breeder or rescue-centre manager will be happy to answer any questions and will offer advice on the care of your new cat. If you are buying a pedigree kitten, always arrange to see the entire litter with the mother, although you are unlikely to be able to see the father as well: queens are usually taken to the stud cats for breeding.

In a rescue centre, you will see many different cats in individual cages. It can be difficult to ignore the plaintive cries of the rescued animals, but prepare yourself to stick rigidly to your original plan for what

Top tip

Unless you can easily take time off from work, don't get a cat on the spur of the moment. He needs your undivided attention while he settles into his new home.

kind of cat you want. If he is not there, then wait a while, or try a different rescue centre. You might live to regret an 'impulse buy'.

Availability

Although kittens are available all year round, the largest number of kittens, especially non-pedigrees, are born in the spring and summer. You may also have to wait for a rescue kitten, as these are in the highest demand at rescue centres, so save some holiday leave ready for when you are able to adopt a cat. Remember that you need to be able to commit to spending at least a week with your new cat, in order to give him the attention he needs to feel safe and loved in his new home.

If you have chosen to buy a pedigree kitten, you should be able to plan well in advance. Once you have reserved your kitten, the breeder will tell you when you can collect him.

Check that the breeder's home is clean and warm. It is a good indication of how well the kittens are cared for.

What to look for in the breeder's house

When you visit the breeder's house to see the kitten, check that it is clean and warm. The litter trays should have been emptied, and the feeding and water bowls scrupulously washed. You can be sure that a warm, comfortable and clean environment is an indication that the cats are also well cared for. If the house, or the area where the cats are kept, is dirty and overcrowded, don't continue with the purchase.

The kittens should be well socialized and used to human contact by the time they are four weeks old. Naturally within a litter, which ranges in size from two to seven kittens, some will be more wary than others. Yet, even after spending a short time with them, all the kittens should be content to play with you and be held without fear. If the kittens appear weak or uninterested, query the reason with the owner. Be wary and don't buy the kitten if you have any doubts about his health, particularly if you have cats at home that could be infected by any disease the kitten may have.

What to ask

The following are the kind of questions you should ask to make sure you get the right cat for your home. Don't be afraid to ask the breeder to explain anything you don't understand relating to cat care; he should be concerned that you have all the knowledge you need to take good care of the kitten.

- What food does the kitten prefer?
- Is he litter-trained and, if so, what kind of litter does he use?
- Has he been socialized with other animals, children and adults?
- Has he been vaccinated?
- Has he been insured?
- Has he been microchipped?
- Has he been neutered and, if not, when is the right time to neuter him?
- Can you contact the breeder if you experience any problems?
- Can you return the kitten if he is unsuitable?

Signs of ill health

Don't be afraid to give the kitten a thorough physical examination. The breeder should expect you to do this and not prevent you from handling the kitten. Many symptoms are easy to spot, even for a novice. The following may indicate an unhealthy kitten:

- A depressed, uninterested demeanour
- A runny nose
- Runny eyes
- Wide pupils (may indicate blindness)
- Sneezing, coughing or wheezing
- A visible haw (third eyelid)
- Excessive earwax or smelly ears
- A swollen abdomen
- A lump on the abdomen (may indicate a hernia)
- A dirty, smelly bottom
- Redness or inflammation of the lips or gums
- Yellow teeth
- Skin sores, dandruff or round bare patches (may indicate ringworm)
- Lameness or unsteadiness
- A kink in the tail
- Deformed legs or feet

Check the kitten for any signs of ill health. In addition, a sick kitten will be lethargic and timid.

Signs of a healthy kitten

The following indicate a healthy kitten:

- A calm but interested demeanour
- A clean mouth with pink gums
- Clean, white teeth
- Clear eyes
- Clean ears
- A clean nose, which is slightly damp and cold
- A shiny, clean coat with no sign of fleas
- A clean bottom
- The kitten walks and runs without difficulty

A healthy kitten will be full of energy and want to play. He will have a shiny coat, bright eyes and a clean bottom.

Top tip

Check the kitten's hearing. When he is not looking at you, click your fingers loudly, or make a noise he should be able to hear, and note the response.

Assessing character

A kitten's 'personality' can indicate how sociable he will be as an adult. The first 2 months of a kitten's life is hugely important in determining his character. During the first 8 weeks, the kitten should be held and played with by a variety of people, including men and children, as well as being introduced to cat-friendly dogs. An outgoing, inquisitive kitten that is not afraid to be held and played with indicates he has been well socialized.

Be wary of a kitten who hides and won't play – he may never enjoy interacting with humans and you may be taking on a cat who spends much of his time running away from you. If you have a family with noisy young children, it would be unfair to introduce a nervous cat into the household. However, such a kitten would appreciate a quiet house with no children – possibly with a single person or a retired couple.

Many people know beforehand what kind of animal they are looking for, but beware – you may want a cat that loves sitting on your lap, but do you want a cat that refuses to sit anywhere else?

Socializing a kitten during the first eight weeks is important if he is to grow into a friendly cat.

Well-being of a rescue cat

If you are getting your cat from a rescue centre, the staff should be able to tell you about him: what they know of his history and health, and how he has been since he has been in their care. Remember that being taken to a rescue centre is a very traumatic experience for a cat, and it can be difficult to assess a cat's character in such conditions. He may be extremely timid while he is in the rescue centre but may be a loving cat once he gets to a new home.

Many rescue centres will ask you to sign a form saying that, if the cat is unsuitable in any way, you will return

A kitten should be inquisitive and responsive to toys. If he hides away, it may indicate an introverted cat that will never become fully socialized.

him to the rescue centre and not pass him on to a third party.

Many people don't give rescue cats enough time to settle into their new home, and return them after a week. Cats need plenty of time to become accustomed to their new environment, particularly if there are other cats or pets to bond with. Allow a few months for your new cat to settle in before deciding whether you want him or not. If there are very serious confrontations that result in injuries, you may have to concede that the new cat is unsuitable and return him to the rescue centre.

CAT BREEDS

There are three sorts of cat – pedigree, non-pedigree and cross-breed (see pages 22–25) – and they come in all shapes, sizes and colours. With many breeds to choose from, ranging in type from the slender elegance of Orientals to the plush cuddliness of British and American Shorthairs, cat fanciers are truly spoilt for choice when it comes to selecting a feline friend.

Good looks

Whether you desire a cat with long hair, short hair, curly hair or even no hair at all, there is bound to be one that fulfils your criteria. Bear in mind, however, that you should not choose a cat on looks alone. You must take into account each breed's character, personality, inherent traits (some of which you may find inconvenient or unacceptable) and the facilities they need to remain sane and sound. Some breeds are very demanding of their owners in terms of the attention they need to remain mentally healthy, while others need a good deal of time spent on their coats on a daily basis to ensure the cat is comfortable.

There's just something about the way they look, behave, feel, move and sound that makes cats so irresistible.

Choosing the right breed

See pages 44–55 for descriptions of the different shapes and colours, and for explanations of commonly used terms. Then use the at-a-glance information provided on pages 56–127, which are devoted to breeds of the world, to assess each breed carefully and see which one has the potential to fit into your lifestyle to your mutual benefit. The only problem that you may encounter is in choosing which type you would like to take home.

Cat breeds

Note

Within the breed descriptions on pages 56–127, the abbreviation ACA stands for the American Cat Association, FIFe stands for the Fédération Internationale Féline and GCCF stands for the Governing Council of the Cat Fancy in the UK.

Shape

While the pedigree breeds are bred true to their particular type, non-pedigrees come in a wide variety of types and conformation owing to their vast mix of genes. There are three basic body shapes – cobby, lithe and muscular – with varieties of tail shape and length, and there are also distinct variations in eye and nose shapes.

Cobby cats

Heads are round, noses short, eyes large and round, and ears small and set wide apart. Chests are broad, legs short and stocky, and paws chunky and round. Tails are substantial at the base and rounded at the tip.

The compact and sturdy British Shorthair is a fine example of a cobby cat.

Unusual tails

Most domestic cats have long tails. However, some breeds feature short tails or no tails at all, owing to a genetic mutation causing spinal malformation. The Japanese Bobtail, for example, features a short, corkscrew tail, 5–10 cm (2–4 in) in length, that can be wagged, flicked, curled and uncurled (unless the vertebrae are fused together, preventing the latter).

Manx cats are 'rumpies', 'stumpies' or 'longies'. The rumpy (true Manx) has no tail at all, while the stumpy (also known as a stubby or riser) bears merely a short stump. Occasionally, a full-tailed kitten (longie or tailed) is born to tailless parents.

The American Bobtail, Pixie-Bob and Kurilian Bobtail are other breeds that feature unusual tails.

Slim and graceful, with long limbs, lithe cat breeds include the Egyptian Mau.

Muscular cats

Generally larger, hardier, stronger and more 'elegant' than their cobby and lithe counterparts, muscular cats have less rounded heads, slightly slanted eyes and ears set closer together. Chests are medium to broad, legs long and strong, and paws substantial and round. Tails taper slightly to a rounded tip.

Lithe cats

These cats are feline ballerinas, since everything about them is sleek, poised and athletic. They tend to be long-bodied and long-limbed with slender legs and compact, oval paws. Head shapes range from wedge-shaped with long noses, slanted, almond-shaped eyes and large triangular ears that are set close together, to more rounded heads and slightly slanted eyes, but again with large ears that are rounded at the tips. Tails are long and taper at the tip.

Well knit and powerfully built, the Maine Coon is one example of a muscularly built feline.

Eye shapes

The four basic eye shapes are:

- Almond
- Oval
- Round
- Slanted (oblique)

Eye shapes and sizes vary widely, however, between breeds.

Clockwise from top left: almond-shaped eyes (Silver Egyptian Mau); oval eyes (Ragdoll); slanted (oblique) eyes (Red Asian Self); round eyes (Korat). For eye colours, see page 52.

Nose shapes

There are four basic feline nose shapes:

- Long
- Medium
- Short (snub nose)
- Full stop (typey nose)

The 'stop' is the term used to describe an extremely short nose. Some breeds have been 'refined' to have stop noses (such as the Peke-faced Persian), but this often leads to respiratory problems (runny eyes and noses) leading to permanently tear-stained facial fur, which is not attractive.

Clockwise from top: Not quite a full stop on this Persian, but almost; Siamese have long noses; British Shorthairs feature short noses; this non-pedigree cat displays a medium-long nose.

Cat breeds

Coat types

Both pedigree and non-pedigree cats can be shorthaired, longhaired or semi-longhaired. Additionally, some pedigree breeds have curly hair of varying length and some are non-coated (apart from a fine down covering the body), but you do not usually find these anomalies in non-pedigrees.

Coat length

Different governing cat councils split breeds of cats into various groups for judging purposes, but to the layman's eye these groupings do not differentiate which breeds are shorthaired, semi-longhaired, longhaired, hairless, or both short- and semi-longhaired. The following list simplifies matters as to which cats have which coat length.

Long

True longhaired cats are typified by their long, dense coats. Breeds in this group include:

- Persian
- Chinchilla

Semi-long

Semi-longhaired cats are those with a less dense coat than Persians. Breeds in this group include:

- Balinese
- Birman
- Maine Coon
- Norwegian Forest
- Siberian
- Oriental Longhair
- Ragdoll
- Turkish Van
- Turkish Angora
- Somali
- Nebelung
- Tiffanie
- Tiffany (Chantilly)
- Cymric
- York Chocolate

Short

- Abyssinian
- Siamese
- Asian Self
- Russian Blue
- Bombay
- British Shorthair
- Burmese
- Burmilla
- Egyptian Mau
- Havana
- Korat
- Ocicat
- Oriental Shorthair
- Cornish Rex
- Devon Rex
- German Rex
- Bengal
- Singapura
- Snowshoe
- American Shorthair
- Tonkinese
- American Wirehair
- Australian Mist
- California Spangled Cat
- Ceylon Cat
- Chartreux
- Chausie
- European Shorthair
- Manx
- Serengeti
- Sokoke
- Savannah
- Anatolian Cat

- Safari Cat
- Toyger
- Keuda
- Exotic Shorthair
- Kanaani

Both short and semi-long

- Non-pedigree
- Scottish Fold
- American Bobtail
- American Curl
- Japanese Bobtail
- Kurilian Bobtail

- LaPerm
- Pixie-Bob
- Selkirk Rex
- Munchkin
- Skookum
- Desert Lynx
- Highland Lynx
- American Ringtail

Hairless

- Sphynx
- Don Sphynx
- Peterbald

Above: This shorthaired Abyssinian cat features a short and plush fur.

Below: The Sphynx is a fine example of a hairless cat; the wrinkles in its skin can be clearly seen.

Coat structure

The feline fur coat is usually made up of three main types of hair:

- Down hairs (undercoat) – the shortest, thinnest and softest hairs. These lie close to the body to conserve the cat's heat.
- Awn hairs (which form the middle coat) – more bristly with a swelling before the tip, which tapers off. These provide insulation and protection.
- Guard hairs (topcoat) – the longest, strongest and thickest. These serve to protect the fur beneath.

The down:awn:guard hair ratio varies greatly between breeds – for example, longhairs have few awn hairs, while wire-coated cats have many. The more awn hairs there are, the 'harsher' the coat is to both sight and touch.

Long

Longhaired cats have an extremely soft, thick and long undercoat covered with an even longer and thicker topcoat. The resulting luxurious coat of uniform length is a dense mass of hair that takes a good deal of grooming to keep it free from tangles and felting (matting). The guard hairs of longhaired cats can be up to ten times longer than that of shorthairs, at up to 12.5 cm (5 in) in length.

Left: This Chinchilla is a true longhair: its fluffy white coat is thick and soft and of even length.

Below: The semi-long coat, displayed here by a Maine Coon cat, is not as dense as that of true longhairs.

Semi-long

The down and guard hairs are shorter than the longhairs', but there are fewer of them so the coats appear less luxurious. Depending on the breed, semi-longhairs can appear shaggy due to uneven lengths of coat, or fine and silky due to the down and guard hairs being less profuse. However long or short their main body hair, all of these cats possess an abundance of inner-ear hair, full tails and fluffy flanks, back legs and, usually, paws.

Short

Shorthaired coats comprise short down and guard hairs of varying thickness depending on the breed. A sprinkling of awn hairs in some cases gives the coat a dense, plush appearance and feel, such as in the British Shorthair. How the coat lies also determines its appearance – flat-lying coats look sleeker.

Curly awn, down and guard hairs all of similar length give curly-coated (rexed) cats their distinctive coats. The American Wirehair was named after its wiry coat featuring individually crimped, hooked or bent hairs.

Hairless

The body is covered with very fine, soft down, which should not be perceptible; there are no awn or guard hairs. Stroking one of these cats is akin to stroking the furred skin of a warm peach. Sometimes there are visible tufts of hair on the face, ears, feet, tail tip and, in males, testicles.

Colours and markings

The range of coat colours and markings in the cat world is astonishing, with pedigrees boasting the most variations. From Red Selfs and Blue Tortie Tabbies to Cinnamon Parti-colours and Apricot Silver Shadeds, cats, it seems, come in almost every available colour scheme there is. Eyes also vary in colour, with odd eyes often being much in demand.

Coat colours and markings

While breeders know what the terms for the various coat colours and markings denote, these fancy names are not always easy for the pet owner to interpret. For example, in layman's terms, a Blue cat is basically a grey one, Lilac is light pinkish grey, Red is ginger and a Black Smoke is a white cat that looks as though it has been playing in a coal bunker!

Eye colours

The eyes are often the most striking feature of cats. Akin to jewels, from a vibrant sapphire-blue to rich amber, the most beautiful of eyes can make even the plainest cat stand out in a crowd.

Eye (iris) colour is genetically controlled. The depth of a particular colour is determined by the amount and type of pigment cells (black, brown or yellow) in the iris. It is the reflected (blue) light on the pigment that produces the colouring. Breed standards call for particular eye colours in varying depths depending on the breed, so breeders carefully mate their cats with the aim of producing the desired eye colour in the resulting kittens.

Eye colours (with breed examples)

Odd eyes – one blue, one orange (Turkish Van)
Orange (British Blue Shorthair)
Yellow (Burmese, Safari Cat)
Golden (American Wirehair, Chausie, Tiffany)
Copper (Black Persian)
Blue (Siamese, Snowshoe, Balinese, Ragdoll)
Green (Russian Blue, Egyptian Mau, Havanna)
Amber (Somali)
Hazel (York Chocolate)

INTERPRETING COLOURS AND MARKINGS

Colour/marking	Description
Apricot	Light pinky brown.
Beige	Pale sandy fawn.
Bi-colour	White coat with dark patches of any recognized colour.
Black	Jet black. Sometimes called Ebony.
Blaze	White strip down nose on dark face.
Blue	Any shade of cold-toned grey; usually slate-grey.
Blue-cream	Mingled or patched coat of pale grey and cream. There are other colour varieties, including Chocolate-cream, Lilac-cream, etc.
Bronze	Warm coppery brown that lightens to buff.
Brown	Any shade of dark brown, except in a brown tabby when it refers to a cat that is genetically black and has black markings on an agouti (grizzled, like a wild rabbit) background. *See* Sable *and* Seal.
Calico	*See* Tortie-and-White.
Cameo	White undercoat with tipped guard hairs of any recognized colour. *See* Tipped.
Caramel	Subtle shade of pale orangey brown.
Champagne	Buff-cream with warm honey-beige shading to pale gold tan.
Chinchilla	Pure white coat with black tipping. *See* Tipped.
Chocolate	Rich, warm brown. Also called Chestnut.
Cinnamon	Light chocolate (also called Light Brown); also Sorrel when referring to Abyssinians.
Colourpoint	White, creamy white or ivory self body with the tail, paws, mask (face) and ears of another colour. Also called Himalayan and Siamese marking.
Cream	Very pale dilute orange (buttermilk).
Dilute	Pale variant of a colour.
Fawn	Light brown (comprising pale cream coat with brown ticking).
Gauntlets	White areas on back paws, which taper up the back of the leg and finish beneath the hocks.
Golden	Pale cream-apricot undercoat with topcoat deepening to gold; light underparts. Back, flanks, head and tail are tipped with brown or black.

Cat breeds

Cat breeds

INTERPRETING COLOURS AND MARKINGS continued

Colour/marking	Description
Harlequin	Black and white bi-colour (also known as Piebald, Tuxedo or Magpie).
Lavender	*See* Lilac.
Lilac	Pale pink-toned dove-grey (dilute of Chocolate). Also sometimes called Platinum (when referring to Burmese), Lavender and Frost.
Mantle	Dark topcoat overlying paler undercoat.
Mink	Range of colours recognized in the USA referring to the Tonkinese breed: natural mink (warm brown with dark chocolate points); champagne mink (soft, warm beige with light brown points); blue mink (soft blue to blue-grey with darker blue points); platinum mink (soft silver with metallic silver points); honey mink (ruddy brown with chocolate points).
Mitted	White paws on dark legs. Often referred to as 'gloves'.
Parti-colour	Bi-colours and torties.
Patched	Two-tone tabby coat with darker and lighter patches, mingling tortie colouring with white or cream and tabby marking. Also called Torbie.
Pewter (blue or black)	Undercoat is light with silvery white topcoat shaded with blue or black.
Platinum	Pale silvery grey with pale fawn undertones.
Points	Colour highlighting the extremities (ears, face, nose, paws and tail).
Red	All shades of ginger. Deep coppery tones are most sought after.
Ruddy	Modification of black in the Abyssinian breed to reddish brown and burnt sienna; known as Usual.
Sable	Dark brown. A term that is sometimes used to describe brown cats that are genetically black.
Seal	*See* Sable.
Self	One colour. Also called Solid.
Shaded	Medium tipping. *See* Tipped.
Shell	Light tipping. *See* Tipped.
Silver	White base hairs with black tipping that give a 'silvered' appearance. Silvering can also occur due to guard hairs having transparent tips.

Colour/marking   Description

Smoke
White undercoat, topcoat hair white at the roots and coloured at the ends. *See* Tipped. Darker points on back, head and feet.

Sorrel
Modification of red in the Abyssinian denoting warm copper undercoat ticked with chocolate.

Spotted
Oval, round or rosette-shaped spots on the body and legs, the tail having narrow rings or spots and the tip being the same colour as the markings. Spotted tabby denotes spots that follow the tabby pattern.

Tabby
There are four basic patterns: ticked (each hair has contrasting dark and light colour bands); mackerel (vertically striped); spotted (as it suggests); and the classic (sides are blotched with whorls or 'oyster' marks). There should be a clearly defined 'M' on the forehead and 'spectacles' around the eyes. Tail is ringed. Front legs have 'broken ring' markings, while the hind legs are barred from front of upper leg to thigh. For brown tabbies, *see* 'Brown'.

Ticking
Two or three bands of colour on the hair shaft as opposed to tipped, which comprises one band of colour.

Tipped
Also known as Tipping or Chinchillation, and usually on guard hairs over a pale or white undercoat. Guard hairs are differently coloured only at the ends, which can create a sparkling effect in some colours. There are three types of tipping – shell (or chinchilla) being the least dense, shaded being medium in density and smoke the most dense.

Torbie
Denotes a coat mingling tabby and tortoiseshell markings or colouring with cream or white. Also known as a Patched Tabby.

Tortoiseshell (Tortie)
Two-coloured (black and red) coat.

Tortie-and-White (Calico)
Tri-coloured (black, red and white).

Van pattern
Predominantly white with patches of colour (usually red or cream) at the base of each ear and the same colour on the tail.

Cat breeds

Abyssinian

intelligent • inquisitive • loyal • gentle • affectionate • agile • playful • talkative

SIZE medium WEIGHT 3–5.5 kg (6½–12 lb) COAT short, fine and close-lying with double ticking at least

LIFESPAN 12+ years

Shorthaired

Abyssinians are believed to be descended from the sacred temple cats of ancient Egypt. They are closely related to the Somali, a semi-longhaired breed, and share many of their characteristics. Abyssinian kittens are lovable and take over their owners' house. They are very talkative and have a trilling voice, much like a bird. They often bond with one person in the house and love to play. Their friendly and trusting nature makes Abyssinians vulnerable, but they need the opportunity to explore so an enclosed garden is essential.

Behavioural characteristics
A true athlete, agile and loves to climb. Enjoys the outdoors and interacting with people. Pines if deprived of human company. Dislikes being confined.

Physical characteristics
Lithe and muscular build, with a slightly rounded, wedge-shaped head. Eyes large, rounded, almond-shaped and expressive. Tufted tips on ears.

Temperament
Likes lots of affection and can be taught tricks, including retrieving balls of paper. Extremely lively.

Colours
Ticked coats in Usual, Sorrel, Blue, Fawn, Chocolate, Lilac (with each having a Silver version), also Tortoiseshell, Red and Cream. Eyes amber, hazel or green.

Perfect owner
A family with time to spend entertaining this intelligent and demanding cat.

Siamese

affectionate • sociable • attention-seeking • energetic • playful • intelligent • inquisitive

SIZE medium   WEIGHT 2–4.5 kg (4½–10 lb)   COAT close-lying, fine, smooth and shiny   LIFESPAN 12+ years

The Siamese is one of the oldest breeds, having originated in Thailand (formerly Siam) hundreds of years ago, where it was prized by royals and the nobility. In Thailand, there is a traditional variety of all-white Siamese known as the Khao Manee ('white jewel'). Khao Manees were reported to have been exported to the USA in recent years, but no further information or breed statistics were available at the time of writing.

Behavioural characteristics
Vocal, lovable and boisterous. Real extrovert, alternately exasperating and enchanting. Loves to run, romp and climb.

Physical characteristics
Long-bodied, lithe, slim and muscular. Wedge-shaped head, large, upright ears and long nose. Almond-shaped, slightly slanted eyes. Long, whippy tail.

Temperament
Loyal and devoted. Most are sociable and good with children, dogs and other cats, but others can become jealous of strangers or other pets.

Colours
The body is pale (ivory, off-white, cream), with the main four point colours being Seal, Blue, Lilac and Chocolate (the only ones recognized as Siamese colours in the USA), but there are many other Solid, Tabby and Torbie point colours (which are all classed as Colourpoint Shorthair in some countries, including the USA). Eyes vivid blue ('Siamese blue').

Perfect owner
Someone who can give this cat a lot of time and attention. Working owners should get another Siamese or Oriental (Siamese tend to overwhelm cats that are less extroverted and demanding than themselves) for company.

Shorthaired

Asian Self European Burmese

outgoing • gentle • loving • energetic • agile • playful • mischievous • loyal

SIZE small to medium WEIGHT 4–5.5 kg (9–12 lb) COAT smooth and close-lying LIFESPAN 12+ years

Shorthaired

Asian Selfs (called European Burmese by some) are cats of Burmese type in colours not accepted for the Burmese breed. Lithe and extremely athletic, these charming cats epitomize understated Eastern elegance and poise. With their 'patent-leather' shine and inscrutable yet 'look at me' appearance, these cats are truly awesome to behold.

Behavioural characteristics
Home-loving, affectionate, confident and boisterous. Extremely sociable with all members of the family and other pets, and can be extremely vocal, especially when he wants a meal. Enjoys being able to explore and play outdoors.

Physical characteristics
Less angular than the Oriental (Foreign) breed and with more rounded, slightly slanted eyes. Solid, athletic and muscular, with medium to large ears set well apart on a rounded head that tapers into a short muzzle. Tail medium to long.

Temperament
Fun-loving, gentle and affectionate. Receptive to leash-training, providing this is done from an early age.

Colours
Available in a rainbow of mouth-watering hues, with sleek, shiny coats showing off the various colours to full effect. Colours are based on those of the Burmese, but are more vibrant (known as 'full expression'). Eye colour depends on coat colour, but generally gold, yellow or green.

Perfect owner
'Perfect for a dog-lover who can't have a dog!' is how one breeder describes this breed. If you want a feline entertainer who is also loving and attentive, this is the cat for you.

Variations

The **Black Asian Self**, perhaps the most popular of all the colour variants, is called the Bombay (and used to be known as the Black American Shorthair and Sable Burmese in the USA) – see page 60.

The **Burmilla** and the **Tiffanie** are, beneath the fur, basically the same cat as the Asian Self – see their separate listings on pages 63 and 107 respectively.

The **Asian Smoke** used to be called the Burmoire.

Russian Blue

hardy • gentle • quiet • placid • affectionate • playful • energetic

SIZE **medium** WEIGHT **2.5–5.5 kg (5½–12 lb)** COAT **soft and dense** LIFESPAN **12+ years**

Russian Blues are thought to have originated in the Russian port of Archangel, near the Arctic Circle. It was not until the late 1940s or early 1950s that great interest was shown in the breed when fresh imports arrived in the USA from the UK. In the 1960s, British breeders sought to re-establish the original breed type.

The coat is easy to maintain – a brush once a week is sufficient to remove loose hairs.

Behavioural characteristics
Greedy with food and prone to unhealthy weight if his diet is not regulated correctly. Bonds with and is devoted to his owner. Agile, enjoys climbing, jumping and racing around.

Physical characteristics
Elegant and graceful. Long and slender, but strong-boned and well muscled. Topcoat stands out from body (like a soft-bristled brush) owing to density of undercoat.

Temperament
Laid-back and sweet-natured. Can be shy with strangers. Good with children, dogs and other cats, but dislikes careless handling or teasing.

Colours
Slate-blue with a silvery sheen (a paler Blue is preferred in the USA); White and Black variants are allowed in some countries (including the UK), known as Russian White and Russian Black. Eyes vivid green.

Perfect owner
Someone who wants a good indoor cat and a loyal, loving companion.

Shorthaired

Bombay

friendly • affectionate • intelligent • energetic • agile • active • sociable • mischievous

SIZE **small to medium** WEIGHT **3.5–5.5 kg (8–12 lb)** COAT **smooth and close-lying** LIFESPAN **12+ years**

Shorthaired

The Bombay (black Asian Self, and also referred to as the 'black Burmese') has several origins: it was created in the USA by mating Burmese with American Shorthairs, and in the UK by accidental matings between Burmese and non-pedigree shorthairs in the 1960s, when the first black kittens were seen.

Bombays' natural curiosity can lead them astray sometimes, so a close eye should be kept on them when outdoors, or they are best kept safely in a large pen will plenty of activity toys to keep them amused. They love to strop their claws, so it is wise to invest in a scratch post; spray it with catnip to encourage your pet to use it, not your furniture.

Behavioural characteristics
As for Asian Self (see page 58).

Physical characteristics
As for Asian Self (see page 58). Surprisingly heavy for his size.

Temperament
As for Asian Self (see page 58). Friendly cat that enjoys all human company, and will happily play with you for hours.

Colours
Jet black with a shimmering patent leather shine. Eyes golden (brilliant copper in the USA), although yellow through to green is acceptable – with deeper colouring preferred.

Perfect owner
An individual or family wanting a feline entertainer who is also loving and attentive.

British Shorthair

quiet • affectionate • friendly • sociable • loyal • devoted • home-loving • playful

SIZE medium to large WEIGHT 4–7 kg (9–15½ lb) COAT crisp, dense and plush LIFESPAN 10+ years

The British Shorthairs (BSH) are the quintessential 'cuddly' cat. Their stocky build and luxuriously plush coats give them a 'teddy bear' appearance. They can take up to 5 years to reach maturity and look their chunky, cuddly best. They require weekly grooming (see pages 143–144) to remove loose hair.

Behavioural characteristics
Happy, willing to please and gentle, sometimes lazy, especially the Blues, and willl put on weight. Keep meal sizes down and do not give treats.

Physical characteristics
Cobby, compact, powerful body with short, strong legs and broad chest. Round face with 'chubby' cheeks. 'Smiling' expression. Short, thick neck and strong, firm, deep chin. Nose short, broad and straight. Eyes large and round and set wide apart. Small ears, rounded at tips. Thick, medium-length tail with rounded tip.

Temperament
Generally excellent. Uncomplicated and easy-going, equally happy to play with humans or curl up on a lap for a cuddle.

Colours
Self-Blue is the best known, and the most popular, of all the colours, closely followed by the Silver Tabby, but the breed now comes in many gorgeous colours including Colourpoint (Himalayan), Self (through the colour spectrum from Cream to Black), Van patterned, Bi-colour, Smoke and Tipped. Eye colours range from copper, yellow, orange or deep gold to sapphire-blue, odd-eyed and hazel or green, depending on the coat colour.

Perfect owner
Any family or individual, and most home environments.

Shorthaired

Burmese

active • intelligent • inquisitive • affectionate • adaptable • friendly • boisterous

SIZE small to medium WEIGHT 3.5–5.5 kg (8–12 lb) COAT close-lying, satiny and glossy LIFESPAN 12+ years

Shorthaired

In the USA, Burmese are bred in two types: traditional and contemporary; the former comprises the UK standard (see 'Physical characteristics'), while the latter calls for a cobbier appearance with rounder eyes and a shorter face. Those cats known as Foreign or European Burmese in some countries are called Asian Selfs in the UK. Browns (sables) are known as Zibelines in France, and as Malayans elsewhere.

Behavioural characteristics
Big personality and vocal. Great entertainer, full of fun and mischief. Hates being alone. Torties are said to be especially mischievous, earning the nickname 'naughty torties'.

Physical characteristics
Hard, muscular, graceful and sleek body. Round head with short nose that has a marked kink in the middle (known as a 'nose break'). Expressive, wide-set, large eyes with the top lid slanting and the bottom lid rounded.

Temperament
Generally excellent, but won't tolerate being teased.

Colours
Brown (sable) is the original colour; also Blue, Chocolate (Champagne), Lilac (Platinum), Red, Cream. Tortie colours are the same except for Red and Cream. Eyes any shade of yellow, from chartreuse to amber, depending on the coat colour.

Perfect owner
Someone who likes an energetic, affectionate and demanding pal who is not afraid to ask for what he wants – and then pester if he does not immediately get it.

Burmilla Asian Shaded

athletic • affectionate • intelligent • playful • gentle • curious • active

SIZE **medium** WEIGHT **3.5–4.5 kg (8–10 lb)** COAT **fine and close-lying** LIFESPAN **12+ years**

This breed resulted from the mating of a Lilac Burmese and a Chinchilla in America in the early 1980s. The kittens featured Burmese type but black-tipped silver coats. Their coats are easy to care for and need a groom only once a week (see pages 143–144).

Behavioural characteristics

Less boisterous than a Burmese but not as laid-back as a Chinchilla. Likes a lot of attention, and will follow you around asking for it.

Physical characteristics

Firm, muscular body with strong, straight back. Modified wedge-shaped head, medium to large ears set well apart and inclined forwards. Medium to long tail. Large, 'kohl-ringed' expressive eyes that are slightly slanted.

⚠ Because they are so friendly, they risk wandering around after strangers if left unattended outside the home.

Temperament

Even-tempered disposition.

Colours

Coats are Agouti (shaded) and tipped with colours seen in the Asian Selfs/Torties. The undercoat is as white as possible in Silver varieties or standard (Golden) in non-Silvers. Eyes from yellow to green, depending on coat colour.

Perfect owner

A person who can set aside plenty of quality time to attend to and play with their pet, and who requires a loyal and devoted companion.

Shorthaired

Egyptian Mau

loving • playful • intelligent • active • energetic • athletic • confident

SIZE **medium** WEIGHT **2.5–5 kg (5½–11 lb)** COAT **close-lying, fine and silky** LIFESPAN **12+ years**

Shorthaired

Stunningly pretty, this breed is believed to have originated in Cairo, but was developed into the Mau we know today by an American breeder of Russian descent in the 1950s. The name 'mau' is the ancient Egyptian word for cat.

Behavioural characteristics
Very playful and needs plenty of mental stimuli – toys and company, either human or feline – to remain happy and healthy. Quick to learn and enjoys doing tricks.

Physical characteristics
Elegant and has a slightly 'worried' look. The ticked coat has a characteristic high sheen and is randomly spotted. Fairly long-bodied and muscular. Eyes large, almond-shaped and slightly slanted. A loose skin flap extends from the flank to the knee on the hind legs.

Temperament
Generally friendly and full of fun. Adores attention and fussing, so makes a good family pet.

Colours
Silver (the best known and most popular), Bronze and Smoke are recognized – all with darker spots and markings. Some breeders are experimenting with other colours, such as Black and Blue. Eyes pale green (called 'gooseberry').

Perfect owner
Family or individual who can provide plenty of company as well as a suitable, safe space to run, climb and play. Egyptian Maus don't like to be left alone for too long, so working people should bear this in mind if intending to get only one cat.

Havana Havana Brown

intelligent • curious • talkative • energetic • agile • affectionate • athletic

SIZE **medium** WEIGHT **3–4 kg (6½–9 lb)** COAT **glossy and fine** LIFESPAN **12+ years**

An Oriental Shorthair, classed in its own right, the Havana is basically an all-brown Siamese with green eyes instead of blue. American Havanas differ from the UK Havana in that they are not as 'Oriental' in type and feature a more squared-off muzzle; outcrossing to Siamese is no longer permitted. The American Havana is, therefore, a different breed to the British Havana (Oriental Self Brown), while the US Oriental Self Brown is the same as the British Havana.

Behavioural characteristics
Likes to make his presence known. Extremely sociable, affectionate and playful, but needs a lot of mental stimulation to remain contented. Does not like to be left alone for long periods. Spirited and inquisitive.

Physical characteristics
Streamlined and heavier than he looks, all muscle. Long, svelte body and long, fine legs. Triangular, long-nosed ('Oriental') head. Large, pricked ears. Long, whippy tail. Slanted, oval ('Oriental') eyes.

Temperament
Loyal, devoted but demanding companion. Adores being stroked and cuddled.

Colours
Rich, warm, deep brown. Vivid green eyes.

Perfect owner
Someone who can provide the company this breed needs. Working owners should get two cats to keep each other company.

Shorthaired

Korat
Si-Sawat/Good-luck Cat/Koraj/Blue Cat of Thailand/Cloud-coloured Cat

playful • quiet • affectionate • agile • gentle • intelligent • energetic

SIZE medium   WEIGHT 2.5–5 kg (5½–11 lb)   COAT sleek and glossy; no undercoat   LIFESPAN 12+ years

Shorthaired

Originating in Thailand some 600 or so years ago, the Korat is one of the world's oldest breeds and is noted for its beautiful, luminous eyes and magical silver-grey coat (referred to as Silver-tipped Blue), with the shimmering effect caused by translucent hair tips. 'Korat' means 'good fortune' in Thai.

Occasionally, Lilac and Blue Colourpoints appear in Korat litters. These variants are called Thais. Only one cat is allowed to carry the Korat name – the traditional Blue one.

Behavioural characteristics
Gregarious and can be talkative when spoken to. Very observant and 'knows what his owner is thinking'. Likes to be involved in what you are doing. Playful.

Physical characteristics
Semi-cobby, strong, lithe and muscular. Heart-shaped face. Short nose with downward curve and slight break. Large, pricked ears. Large, 'oversized' eyes that look rounded when fully open but slanted when fully or partially closed.

Temperament
Loving, loyal, relaxed and good-natured. Sociable with dogs and other, more docile, cats.

Colours
Any shade of Blue (grey) with the characteristic sheen achieved by silver-tipped guard hairs. Brilliant green (peridot) eyes (an amber cast is often seen and is acceptable). Kittens often have amber eyes which turn green as they get older.

Perfect owner
Someone wanting a loving and gentle, devoted companion.

Ocicat

affectionate • sociable • agile • energetic • vocal • hardy • extrovert

SIZE **medium to large** WEIGHT **2.5–6.5 kg (5½–14 lb)** COAT **close-lying, satiny and sleek** LIFESPAN **12+ years**

The Ocicat was developed in the 1960s by crossing Siamese with Abyssinians, and adding American Shorthairs later to produce size and the Silver colour range. A Jungala is simply the Classic Tabby-patterned Ocicat, which comes in the same colours as its spotted counterpart.

Behavioural characteristics
Playful and confident, yet undemanding. No problems.

Physical characteristics
Large, but agile, athletic and very graceful. Extremely fluid movement when playing and hunting.

Temperament
Loves people and enjoys their company; dislikes being left on his own. Good with children, dogs and other cats.

Colours
All spotted: Tawny (Brown Spotted Tabby), Blue (and Silver), Chocolate (and Silver), Lilac (Lavender; and Silver), Cinnamon (and Silver), Fawn (and Silver), Silver and Black Silver. Eyes any colour except blue.

Perfect owner
Someone who can provide plenty of space and facilities to entertain this cat and fulfil his natural feline instincts. If denied outside access for safety reasons, he will be quite happy indoors.

Shorthaired

Oriental Shorthair

intelligent • curious • talkative • energetic • agile • affectionate • athletic

SIZE medium   WEIGHT 3–4 kg (6½–9 lb)   COAT glossy and fine   LIFESPAN 12+ years

Shorthaired

During the development of the Havana (Self Brown Siamese) in the 1950s, other 'side product' Self and non-Self (Tortie, Smoke, Shaded and Tabby) colours were produced; these were called Foreigns and Orientals, respectively. With the exception of the Havana and Foreign White (whose UK breed clubs wanted to retain the names), the UK's main cat organization deemed that all other Siamese cats of non-pointed colouring were Orientals.

In the USA, however, Havanas differ from UK Havanas in that they are not as 'Oriental' in type and feature a more squared-off muzzle; outcrossing to Siamese is not permitted (which limits the gene pool). The American Self Brown that followed the British Havana breeding is known as the Oriental Self Brown, while American Foreign Whites are known as Oriental Whites in the UK.

The Seychellois was an experimental Van-type patterned Oriental breed during the 1980s (both short- and semi-longhaired) that appears to have fizzled out.

Behavioural characteristics
Extremely sociable, affectionate and playful, but needs a lot of mental stimulation to remain contented. Does not like to be left alone.

Physical characteristics
Streamlined and heavier than he looks, all muscle. Long, svelte body and long, fine legs.

Temperament
Makes a loyal, devoted but demanding companion that adores being stroked and cuddled.

Colours
Many fabulous colours in Selfs, Torties, Smokes and Shadeds. Eyes green, but brilliant blue in Whites (green is allowed in the USA).

Perfect owner
Someone who has plenty of time to spend with their cat. Working owners are advised to get two cats so they can keep each other company.

friendly • affectionate • intelligent • sociable • playful • lively • devoted

SIZE **small to medium**   WEIGHT **2–4 kg (4½–9 lb)**   COAT **wavy and silky**   LIFESPAN **12+ years**

The term 'rex' refers to a cat with a curly coat, and rexed cats have been recorded since the early 1930s in East Prussia (Germany), although they are also to be seen on Victorian postcards. The distinctive coat is due to a normally recessive gene (which means that both parents have to carry it for the kittens to have curly coats); in other rexed breeds the gene is dominant.

The origination of the Cornish Rex dates back to the 1950s when a curly-coated kitten named Kallibunker was born to a domestic barn cat in Cornwall, England. His owner mated him back to his mother, more curly coats were produced and a breeding programme developed. A pregnant queen was exported to the USA in the late 1950s to found the breed there.

The Si-Rex is a Cornish or Devon Rex crossed with Siamese to achieve Siamese colouring and points. Some countries and cat organizations class them as a separate breed.

Behavioural characteristics

Quite vocal. Lively and nimble, enjoys climbing, leaping and sprinting. Clever, adept at opening cupboard doors. Seeks out warm places to rest and sit.

Physical characteristics

Elegant and graceful. Slender, but hard and muscular. Curly whiskers and eyebrows. Large, oval eyes and large, upright ears. Naturally arched back and 'tucked up' underbody. Taller and finer-boned than the Devon Rex. The coat should be dense without any bald patches.

Temperament

Perky, home-loving. Bonds strongly with his owner and adores being petted and cuddled by all members of the family. Good with children, dogs and other cats.

Colours

Any colours and markings permitted, including Colourpoint (Si-Rex). Eyes any colour.

Perfect owner

Someone wanting an affectionate indoor cat that is soft and warm to cuddle. For outdoor exercise, an enclosed large run is preferable, with toys and scratching and climbing facilities. A warm environment is essential.

Shorthaired

Devon Rex Butterfly Rex

friendly • extrovert • quiet • playful • affectionate • intelligent • inquisitive

SIZE **small to medium** WEIGHT **2–4.5 kg (4½–10 lb)** COAT **wavy and soft** LIFESPAN **12+ years**

Shorthaired

The Devon Rex originated in Devon, England, in 1960, when a curly-coated kitten named Kirlee was born to a stray non-pedigree female and her stray curly-coated suitor. Kirlee was mated with Cornish Rex females, but only straight-coated kittens resulted; only inbreeding produced curly fur. So the gene responsible for the curl was determined to be different to that of the Cornish Rex, although these genes are recessive in both breeds.

The Devon Rex has a thinner, slightly coarser curly coat (a few short guard hairs are present) than the Cornish Rex (see page 69) but with a sturdier body and different facial appearance – some say it looks 'impish', like a pixie. The Devons were outcrossed at various times with British and American Shorthairs and Burmese.

The Devon Rex's habit of wagging his tail when happy earned him the nickname 'poodle cat' (not to be confused with the Poodle Cat [Pudelkatze] – an experimental breed now believed to be extinct).

Behavioural characteristics
Home-loving and adores attention. Attracted to warm places. Extremely active and loves to play with toys, climb and leap.

Physical characteristics
Medium-long, muscular, slender body. Curly whiskers and eyebrows. Slightly shorter and heavier-boned than the Cornish Rex.

Temperament
Extremely sociable and good with children, dogs and other cats. Needs lots of attention from his owner, and a warm environment.

Colours
Any coat and eye colour acceptable.

Perfect owner
As for the Cornish Rex.

German Rex

extrovert • inquisitive • playful • intelligent • affectionate • quiet • gentle
SIZE small to medium   WEIGHT 3–5 kg (6½–11 lb)   COAT soft, thick, silky and wavy/curly   LIFESPAN 10+ years

The breed was founded in the 1950s in Berlin, Germany. However, it had virtually died out by 1999, so a group of dedicated breeders got together to re-establish a breeding programme, which is now flourishing.

It appears that the Oregon and California varieties of rexed cat that have been reported (but apparently are not being bred any longer) had the same gene as the German Rex. One cat, a black and white rexed stray called the 'Sieburg Rex' in Germany, contributed to the German Rex gene pool in 1979.

Behavioural characteristics
Lively and enjoys climbing, running and leaping. Clever and curious, likes to be involved in everything his owner does, and if bored soon finds his own entertainment in which to involve his owner. Adores being cuddled and petted.

Physical characteristics
Comparable in conformation to a European Shorthair (see page 83). Curly whiskers and eyebrows. Same height as the Cornish Rex (see page 69), but more heavily built and well-muscled, with a thicker coat.

Temperament
Ultra-affectionate, friendly and sociable. Good with children, dogs and other cats.

Colours
All coat and eye colours; blue is preferred for Si-Rex and bright green for Selfs.

Perfect owner
A family or individual who can provide a warm environment and plenty of human company, so not ideal for full-time working people, unless they have two cats.

Shorthaired

Bengal

intelligent • alert • active • confident • sociable • talkative • playful

SIZE **medium to large**   WEIGHT **4.5–9 kg (10–20 lb)**   COAT **thick, silky and soft**   LIFESPAN **12+ years**

Shorthaired

The Bengal originated in the USA as a result of crossing a non-pedigree shorthaired cat with an Asian Leopard Cat (a wild species of feline). This hybrid was known as an F1; later generations became known as F2, F3, F4, F5 and so on. F1s, F2s and F3s tend to retain their wild instincts.

Behavioural characteristics
Loves to play with water, so a water feature is a good idea. Thrives in a mentally and physically stimulating environment and enjoys the company of humans, dogs and other cats.

Physical characteristics
Sleek, long, muscular and athletic.

Temperament
F4s onwards generally make good pets, but can present challenging behaviour at times if something or their lifestyle does not suit them. Will roam if unchecked, so a cat-safe yard or garden, or a large outdoor cat pen, is essential.

Colours
In the UK, there are the Brown (Black), both Spotted and Marbled, with gold, green or hazel eyes, and two types of Snow, both Spotted and Marbled – one with blue eyes and the other with gold, green or blue-green eyes. The Browns (Blacks) have a rufous base coat (yellow, buff, golden or orange) with brown or black spots (Spotted) or streaks (Marbled); the Snows have an ivory or cream base coat with charcoal or brown spots or streaks.

In the USA, Bengal colours and markings are referred to as Leopard (with black spots on an orange background); Mink (with black spots on a mahogany background); and Sorrel (with brown spots on a light orange background). Eyes gold, green or hazel.

Perfect owner
A very experienced cat owner with a good understanding of feline behaviour, along with plenty of safe space, both inside and out.

Singapura Kucinta/Drain Cat/River Cat

affectionate • friendly • playful • intelligent • home-loving • mischievous • devoted

SIZE small to medium   WEIGHT 2–4 kg (4½–9 lb)   COAT fine, dense and close-lying   LIFESPAN 10+ years

Controversy surrounds the origination of the Singapura, regarding whether it is an ancient and truly native type of cat that was discovered in Singapore by an American couple in the 1970s and introduced into the USA by them, or whether it was 'manufactured' by crossing Burmese and/or Abyssinians in their home country. It used to be the smallest breed of cat, but outcrossing to expand the gene pool has increased its size.

Behavioural characteristics
Kitten-like throughout adulthood. Very playful and interactive, adores human company. Dislikes cold and wet weather. Likes to climb to high observation points.

Physical characteristics
Muscular and lithe, heavier than he looks, with noticeably large ears and 'owl-like' eyes. 'Sparkling' appearance due to ticked coat. Blunt-tipped tail. Round head with short nose and slight 'break'.

Temperament
Good-natured, gentle and playful.

Colours
One colour only: Sepia Agouti; the main body colour is Old (golden) Ivory ticked with Dark Brown. Eyes, nose and lips are 'kohl-lined' in dark brown and there should be a 'Cheetah' line from inside the inner corner of the eye to just behind the whisker pads. Salmon-coloured nose. Eyes hazel, green or yellow.

Perfect owner
Anyone wanting a loving companion or lap cat to live indoors.

Shorthaired

Snowshoe Silver Laces

intelligent • playful • affectionate • talkative • agile • sociable • easy-going
SIZE medium to large WEIGHT 2.5–5.5 kg (6–12 lb) COAT close-lying, medium-coarse and glossy LIFESPAN 10+ years

Shorthaired

Created in the USA in the late 1960s by crossing Siamese with a Bi-coloured American Shorthair, the Snowshoe is a spectacular-looking cat combining Siamese beauty with American Shorthair bulk. While not recognized by the UK's official cat organization, the GCCF, the pretty Snowshoe is nevertheless a popular breed, albeit more so in the USA, where it is officially recognized (the only country where it is) and is shown at Championship status.

Behavioural characteristics

Active and athletic, this lively cat enjoys interactive games with owners. Enjoys toys, running and leaping, so must have enough space and facilities to do so. Being highly interactive, prefers company most of the time.

Physical characteristics

Looks like a heavily built, more rounded Siamese, but retains elegance and grace. Distinctive white paws.

Temperament

Equable, calm and loves being petted. Good with children, dogs and other cats. Extremely companiable but more laid-back and less noisy than Siamese.

Colours

Blue and Seal Point are recognized, but other Siamese colours are now being bred, including Lilac and Chocolate. Two colour patterns, both with white paws ('gloves' on front and 'shoes' on back): Mitted comprises Siamese (Himalayan) pattern with up to a third of the body being white excluding the face; Bi-colour comprises up to two-thirds of the body being white, including the nose. Eyes blue.

Perfect owner

Those wanting an ideal indoor pet, as he likes home comforts and lots of attention.

American Shorthair

powerful • confident • hardy • low-maintenance • easy-going • affectionate • agile

SIZE medium to large WEIGHT 3–5.5 kg (6½–12 lb) COAT thick, even and of hard texture LIFESPAN 12+ years

The American Shorthair's ancestors came to North America with early European settlers, and some arrived with the Pilgrim Fathers on the *Mayflower*. Formerly known as the Domestic Shorthair, which now refers to non-pedigree shorthairs in the States, American Shorthairs were selectively bred from non-pedigrees until they bred true to a type, and remained so.

An efficient rodent exterminator when he gets the opportunity, the American Shorthair is a tough 'working cat' that generally enjoys good health and few behavioural problems. They make good family pets and are adaptable to many home situations.

Behavioural characteristics
Independent, energetic, companiable when he wants to be. Enjoys hunting and the opportunity to explore and play outside.

Physical characteristics
Strong, athletic, muscular and well-proportioned, natural rather than contrived appearance. Less cobby than the British Shorthair but stockier than the European Shorthair. Eyes large, wide-set and slightly slanted, the upper lid having an almond-shaped curve and the lower lid being rounded.

Temperament
Generally placid and friendly. Equally at home in the farmyard or curled up in front of the fire.

Colours
Most Self, Shaded, Cameo, Silver, Smoke, Tabby, Bi- and Parti-colours and Van patterns accepted. Lilac, Chocolate and Colourpointed not encouraged. Eyes brilliant gold in most coat colours.

Perfect owner
Someone who does not want a permanently 'clingy' pet, or who needs a cat to assist with rodent control on a farm or smallholding.

Shorthaired

Tonkinese

intelligent • sociable • loyal • affectionate • active • playful • outgoing

SIZE medium WEIGHT **2.5–5 kg (5½–11 lb)** COAT **close-lying, fine, soft and silky** LIFESPAN **12+ years**

Shorthaired

Affectionately nicknamed the 'Tonks', the Tonkinese is a cross between Burmese and Siamese and was developed in the USA during the 1950s. It was named after the Gulf of Tonkin, which is located near Myanmar (formerly Burma) and Thailand (formerly Siam). At one time the breed was nicknamed the 'Golden Siamese'.

Behavioural characteristics
Energetic, gregarious and adores human company. Does not thrive when lonely. Fun-loving and wants to be involved in everything that is going on. Enjoys running, leaping and climbing.

Physical characteristics
Muscular, sleek and elegant, combining the lithe grace of the Siamese with Burmese strength. Coat comprises a subtle merging of toning colour from point shades to body shade, rather than being sharply defined.

Temperament
Very affectionate and loyal. Good with children, dogs and other cats.

Colours
Wide variety of Solid, Colourpointed, Tortie and Tabby colours that include Brown, Blue, Chocolate, Lilac, Red, Cream, Caramel and Apricot; Mink (USA) shades comprise Natural, Champagne, Blue, Platinum and Honey. Eyes greenish blue to bluish green (aquamarine to turquoise).

Perfect owner
Those who can provide full-time loving company, lots of mental stimulation and physical interaction, as well as plenty of indoor space or a large, secure, outdoor pen.

American Wirehair

friendly • intelligent • sturdy • adaptable • powerful • inquisitive • confident

SIZE **medium to large** WEIGHT **3.5–5 kg (8–11 lb)** COAT **springy, dense and coarse** LIFESPAN **12+ years**

American Wirehairs originated in the 1960s in America. Outcrossing to American Shorthairs strengthened the breed. Awn, down and guard hairs are all individually twisted, while the awn hairs are hooked at the ends, producing the distinctive coat. Even the whiskers are curly or wavy. The wirehaired coat needs only a weekly brush (see pages 143–144) to remain in good condition.

Behavioural characteristics
Undemanding attention-wise compared to some other breeds, but enjoys a good deal of activity both inside and out. Agile and curious.

Physical characteristics
Almost identical to the American Shorthair (see page 75), but with a wiry coat that feels coarse, rather like lamb's wool. Eyes large and round.

Temperament
Quiet, reserved, loving. Purrs a lot.

Colours
All colours and patterns with a few exceptions. Eyes usually brilliant gold, but any colour is accepted as long as it relates to coat colour – generally deep blue, odd-eyed, green, blue-green or hazel.

Perfect owner
A cat lover who appreciates something completely different.

Shorthaired

Australian Mist

ultra-affectionate • gentle • playful • intelligent • alert • attentive • inquisitive

SIZE **medium** WEIGHT **4–7 kg (9–15½ lb)** COAT **dense and soft** LIFESPAN **12+ years**

Shorthaired

The Australian Mist (formerly known as the Spotted Mist) was developed in Australia in 1977 by Dr Truda Straede, who crossed Burmese, Abyssinian and non-pedigree shorthairs to produce kittens with distinctive spotted coats on a ticked background. Later, kittens appeared in the breeding programme with marbled coats, so the two types – Spotted Mist and Marbled Mist – now go under the one banner of Australian Mist.

Behavioural characteristics
Particularly affectionate with people and enjoys the company of other cats and pets. Happy to play with toys and participate in games. Retains a kittenish element throughout life. Extremely people-orientated, home-loving and content to remain indoors.

Physical characteristics
Well-muscled breed of somewhat foreign type, due to its Abyssinian and Burmese ancestors. Non-pedigree genes provide an element of hardiness and vitality. Broad, rounded head with large, almond-shaped eyes.

Temperament
Extremely affectionate and tolerant, making a wonderful family pet. Gets on well with other pets.

Colours
Brown, Blue, Chocolate, Lilac, Gold or Peach spots or 'marbles' set on a 'misty' background that is creamy mushroom. Legs and tails are ringed or barred, with lines of colour on the face and neck. Eyes green.

Perfect owner
Family, someone who works from home or an elderly person who requires a loving, gentle companion. Suited to being a wholly indoor cat, so would be ideal for people without outdoor facilities.

California Spangled Cat

lively • energetic • affectionate • sociable • gentle • intelligent

SIZE **medium**   WEIGHT **3.5–7 kg (8–15½ lb)**   COAT **soft, longer on belly and tail**   LIFESPAN **unspecified**

This is a rare breed created by Paul Casey, a Hollywood screenwriter, to resemble the leopard. He mixed spotted and tabby Oriental types with non-pedigrees. In 1996 his California Spangled Cat was presented to two million potential buyers in Neiman-Marcus' (an exclusive American department store) Christmas catalogue at a price of $1,400 each. Casey felt that this 'stunt' would bring attention to the plight of big cats killed for their fur, but in fact it caused much controversy with the breed being dubbed a designer gimmick. Today there are few breeders and there is a concern that the California Spangled Cat will die out.

Behavioural characteristics
Equally at home indoors or out. No major problems.

Physical characteristics
Looks 'wild' but is in fact totally domesticated. Gives the impression of being bigger than it actually is due to its 'leopard spotting'. Athletic and enjoys interaction with humans.

Temperament
Good-tempered.

Colours
Silver (Snow Leopard), Charcoal, Bronze, Gold, Blue, Red, Brown and Black. Eyes gold to brown; blue in Silvers.

Perfect owner
Someone who wants a rare breed, is prepared to wait until they find one, and pay a vast amount of money for the privilege.

Shorthaired

Ceylon Cat
Gatto di Ceylon/Ceylonese/Celonese/Sri Lankan Cat

sociable • friendly • attractive • energetic • playful • alert • agile • elegant

SIZE small to medium   WEIGHT 2–4.5 kg (4½–10 lb)   COAT close-lying, fine and silky; sparse undercoat
LIFESPAN 13+ years

Shorthaired

With colouring and conformation very similar to the Abyssinian, the Ceylon Cat owes its origin to the Cat Club of Sri Lanka (formerly Ceylon), who developed it from a non-pedigree type in the country. An Italian veterinary surgeon, Dr Paolo Pellegata, took some of these cats back to Italy with him in the 1980s, with the aim being to fix the breed type. While they have grown in popularity in Italy, this breed is rare elsewhere. To retain the breed's unspoiled features, the Italian Club Amatori del Gatto di Ceylon recommends that a natural Ceylon Cat born in Sri Lanka is introduced to a breeding programme every four or five generations.

Behavioural characteristics
No major problems. Inquisitive, playful, affectionate, yet also quite independent. Likes to curl up in warm places near his owner.

Physical characteristics
Compact and well muscled but with fine bone structure. Large, slightly slanted, 'eyelined' eyes with rounded lower lid and almond-shaped top lid, giving the breed's characteristic 'dreamy' expression.

Temperament
Sociable and trusting.

Colours
The original, and most typical, sandy-golden ticked background with black ticking is known as Manilla colouring. The base colour can range through various shades of ash, honey, sand, cinnamon, orange-pekoe, ginger, pearl and jet-black. Ash colouring is known locally by Singalese as 'Alu Patu', and 'Dumburu Pata' is a warmer, brown shade. Ticking and markings can also be in the new colours of Blue, Red, Cream or Tortie. Barred leg markings and a ringed tail. Eyes from yellow to green.

Perfect owner
An individual or family who can offer plenty of time and facilities to entertain this energetic breed, which thrives on affection and mental stimulation.

Chartreux Chartreuse/Certosino/Karthhauser/Karthuizer

calm • agile • intelligent • playful • powerful • sociable • quiet

SIZE medium to large   WEIGHT 3–5.5 kg (6½–12 lb)   COAT very dense, soft and plush   LIFESPAN 10+ years

Virtually identical to the British Blue Shorthair, but not as cobby and lighter in weight, the Chartreux is a French breed. These cats reach full maturity at 3–4 years of age. Owing to the outcrossing to Persians many years ago, there are occasional incidences of semi-longhaired Chartreux cats in litters. Enthusiasts have called these beautiful cats Benedictines.

Behavioural characteristics
Renowned for quietness. Playful (will even retrieve toys), intelligent, and loves to hunt given the opportunity. Dedicated to owner, and dog-like in devotion and behaviour. Amenable with dogs and other cats, and gentle with children, but will not tolerate teasing.

Physical characteristics
Sturdy, solid-boned and well muscled. Extremely agile and energetic for its size. 'Smiling' expression. Eyes large and round.

Temperament
Generally gentle and affectionate, enjoys interacting and playing with owner. Deceptively 'lazy', turning into a fierce predator when hunting.

Colours
Any shade of Blue with silver highlights. Eyes gold to copper, with deep, brilliant orange preferred.

Perfect owner
Someone looking for a cheerful house cat that adores the chance to play and explore outside; a cat-safe garden is the ideal.

Shorthaired

Chausie

alert • intelligent • sociable • athletic • agile • fast • muscular

SIZE **medium to large** WEIGHT **average 7 kg (15½ lb)** COAT **coarse to fine and smooth** LIFESPAN **12+ years**

A new breed developed in the USA in the 1990s, the Chausie is a result of the African Jungle Cat (*Felis chaus*) being crossed with non-pedigree shorthairs. Third-generation (F3) Chausies are considered suitable for pets; the first (F1) and second (F2) generations are too wild. They make good indoor pets as long as they have the run of the house. Outside play areas are good as long as the enclosure is escape-proof.

Behavioural characteristics

Rarely sits still in one place for long. 'Dog-like' in manner. Very energetic, especially in first year, and needs room to run and climb.

Physical characteristics

Tall, long-legged, lean and long. Speedy, and can jump up to 2 m (6 ft) in a vertical leap. Large, tufted ears. Eyes almond-shaped and slanted. Nose medium in length with a definite break.

Temperament

Not afraid of much. Sweet-natured, affectionate and amenable with dogs and other cats if brought up and socialized correctly. (There may be a problem introducing dogs and other pets to an older Chausie.)

Colours

Brown-ticked Tabby, Melanistic (Black) and Silver-tip Melanistic. Eyes golden.

Perfect owner

Someone who can afford to buy this expensive breed, and has plenty of indoor space for him to run and play, or an outdoor pen.

⚠ Buy only from a reputable breeder.

European Shorthair

adaptable • hardy • confident • low-maintenance • easy-going • affectionate • agile

SIZE medium to large   WEIGHT 3–5.5 kg (7–12 lb)   COAT close-lying, dense, glossy and springy

LIFESPAN 12+ years

Originally brought to Denmark, Sweden and Finland by the Romans, Vikings and merchant traders, the European Shorthair developed over the centuries in much the same way as the American and British Shorthairs. Non-pedigrees were selectively bred by enthusiasts until these bred true to a type and remained so, becoming recognized as a breed in the early 1980s. Today this is one of the most popular shorthaired breeds in Scandinavia – a robust and healthy breed that presents few problems to owners.

Behavioural characteristics

Adept and enthusiastic hunter that enjoys being outside given the chance. Playful. Some learn to be 'chatty' if their owners talk to them; otherwise quiet. Agile and alert. Enjoys climbing.

Physical characteristics

Strong and muscular, natural-looking cat. Not cobby like the British Shorthair, nor as compact as the American Shorthair. Large head that is longer than it is wide. Medium-length, slightly indented nose, and medium-sized ears (sometimes tufted). Medium-length, powerful legs and round paws. Large, round eyes that are slightly slanted.

Temperament

Has a mind of his own, but generally sweet, gentle and companiable. Equally at home in town or country. Good with children, dogs and other cats.

Colours

There are 69 recognized colours including Selfs, Smokes, Tortie, Tabby, Bi-colour, Harlequin and Van pattern. Eyes green, amber, blue or odd-eyed (blue and amber), depending on the coat colour.

Perfect owner

Family or individual wanting an independent yet affectionate pet.

Shorthaired

Manx

laid-back • placid • intelligent • quiet • loyal • affectionate • courageous • strong

SIZE **medium** WEIGHT **3.5–5.5 kg (8–12 lb)** COAT **thick, fluffy and double** LIFESPAN **10+ years**

Shorthaired

This tailless breed is hundreds of years old. Originating on the Isle of Man, in the Irish Sea between Ireland and England, where they are still being bred and are the island's emblem, there are many legends as regards how the Manx came to have no tail. However, this is due to a genetic mutation. See page 109 for a full description, as shorthaired Manx are just the same as the Cymric (longhaired Manx), apart from the length of coat. Show Manx must have no tail (rumpies), but stumpies and longies are used for breeding, and all types make good pets.

Behavioural characteristics
See page 109. Very dog-like in many habits, such as chasing, retrieving and burying toys. Makes a distinctive 'trilling' sound when talking to kittens or owner. Likes to jump as well as climb.

Physical characteristics
See page 109.

Temperament
Generally excellent (see page 109).

Colours
See page 109. While colour and markings carry no points in the UK, the coat texture is worth up to 20 points. Chocolate, Lavender and Colourpoint (Himalayan) colouring, or these colours with White, are not allowed by some cat associations.

Perfect owner
See page 109. Manx make good family pets.

Serengeti

affectionate • sociable • friendly • vocal • intelligent • lively • energetic

SIZE medium to large   WEIGHT 3.5–6.5 kg (9–14 lb)   COAT fine, dense and moderately soft
LIFESPAN 10+ years

Developed by Karen Sausman in California in 1994, the Serengeti comprises a cross between Oriental Shorthairs and Bengals. The aim was to create a temperamentally sound household pet that looked like the African Serval without introducing wild blood into the equation. Registered with The International Cat Association (TICA) as a developing breed, Serengetis are still relatively rare, but their popularity is increasing as more of these cats are becoming available to the public.

Behavioural characteristics
Loves to be involved with whatever his owner is doing. Clever and resourceful. Quite demanding of time and attention. Very vocal and chatty, with a wide vocabulary of sounds. Likes to run, leap and climb, so must have space and facilities to do so.

Physical characteristics
Long, lean body, long neck, long legs, narrow face, big ears and spotted coat. Similar in looks and conformation to the Oriental Shorthair (see page 68) but squarely built and altogether larger and bigger-boned. Large, round eyes. Very upright posture. Strong and muscular, yet graceful.

Temperament
Gentle, outgoing, confident and alert. Described as 'sweet-natured, extremely affectionate and the ultimate house cat' by one breed enthusiast. Sociable with children, dogs and other cats.

Colours
Clear Yellow (Cold Tan) to Gold (Warm Tan) Tabby with a pattern of widely spaced Black or Dark Brown spots, Solid Black with/without 'ghost' spots, Silver with Black spots, and Black Smoke. Some coats have a 'glitter' effect. 'Teardrop' markings on face desirable. Eyes ideally copper or gold, but yellow and green shades are permitted at the moment.

Perfect owner
Someone looking for lots of character and personality in a cat. Not for those who want a quiet, laid-back pet.

Shorthaired

Sokoke Sokoke Forest Cat/Kadzonzo

playful • affectionate • agile • athletic • self-assured • independent • intelligent

SIZE medium   WEIGHT 2.5–5.5 kg (5½–12 lb)   COAT close-lying, dense, springy and shiny; no undercoat
LIFESPAN 11+ years

Shorthaired

The breed originates from the Sokoke Arabuke Forest in Kenya, Africa. The earliest knowledge of them comes from the ancient Giriama tribe, who call them 'Kadzonzo' ('looks like tree bark'), and who used to eat them rather than their livestock, which represented wealth. The Denmark-based International Sokoke Society continues to import potential breeding stock from Kenya. In 2004, there were 31 breeding pairs spread throughout Denmark, Norway, Sweden, the UK and France.

Behavioural characteristics
Quite independent and proud, but enjoys human company. Talkative, playful and interactive. Does not like to be hugged or held tightly. Acts more like a dog than a cat. Males play a large part in raising kittens.

Physical characteristics
Looks similar to an ocelot. Muscular, lean, slender body with strong bone structure. Modified wedge-shaped head with almost straight nose and, ideally, lynx-tufted ears. Long legs. Almond-shaped, slightly slanted eyes.

Temperament
Does not enjoy being 'coddled', but always ready to be petted and curl up on a lap when he chooses. Bonds strongly with owner and is devoted. Thrives in groups and gets on with other cats. Needs lots of space to run, jump and climb, and toys to play with.

Colours
African Tabby pattern comprises a sandy base colour with 'blotched' Tabby pattern markings ranging from Light Brown to Dark Chestnut. No white hairs. Eyes 'kohl-lined' and various shades of amber to light green. The few Snow Sokokes born so far have cream to grey-beige markings, a 'masked' face and blue eyes.

Perfect owner
Someone able to provide a quiet, warm, indoor life. A hectic, chaotic household will not suit Sokokes, nor will small children.

Savannah

friendly • talkative • intelligent • playful • inquisitive • athletic • agile

SIZE **large** WEIGHT **4.5–9 kg (10–20 lb)** COAT **close-lying and slightly coarse** LIFESPAN **10+ years**

Savannahs originated in the USA in the mid-1980s, when a domestic shorthair was crossed with an African Serval. Further early generations of Savannahs were created by outcrossing to non-pedigrees, Oriental Shorthairs, Egyptian Maus, Serengetis and Bengals.

Behavioural characteristics
Likes to romp and play, and needs plenty of toys and attention to maintain mental health. Enjoys playing with water.

Physical characteristics
Large, long-bodied, 'wild-looking' and graceful, with beautiful spotted or striped coat and 'teardrop' markings around the eyes.

Temperament
Sweet-natured, affectionate, loyal and sociable with children, dogs and other cats.

Colours
Black, Black Smoke, Brown Spotted Tabby and Silver Spotted Tabby. Eyes should be yellow, gold, green or caramel brown, whatever the coat colour.

Perfect owner
Someone who is willing to provide lots of attention, affection and interaction. Plenty of indoor space and play facilities are required and, preferably, a secure outdoor exercise or play pen.

⚠ A first-generation (filial) cross (F1), like the Bengal (see page 72), tends to be much more active and less suited to be an average domestic family pet than the later crosses (F2s and later).

Shorthaired

Anatolian Cat Turkish Shorthair/Anadolu Kedisi/Van Kedi

affectionate • agile • powerful • gentle • energetic • inquisitive • friendly

SIZE medium to large WEIGHT 4–6.5 kg (9–14 lb) COAT dense, close-lying and crisply soft

LIFESPAN 12+ years

Naturally originating in Turkey hundreds of years ago, the Anatolian is currently being standardized by enthusiasts – via outcrossing with Turkish Vans to enlarge the gene pool – who are trying to achieve breed recognition under the name of Turkish Shorthair. Blue-eyed whites are predisposed to deafness (a fact that is also true of the same colouring in other breeds).

In their native country, all-white Anatolians and Turkish Vans with blue eyes are known as Van Kedi, because the Turks do not differentiate between the all-white short- and semi-longhaired varieties.

⚠ Care should be taken to run baths cold, before adding hot water, in case these cats get into the bathroom, jump into the water and scald themselves; it is also a good idea to keep toilet lids down.

Behavioural characteristics

Possibly even more attracted to water than the Turkish Van (see page 103). Very energetic, fast and great leaper. Devoted to owner, and pines if he does not get enough attention.

Physical characteristics

Strong and muscular, with leg length in proportion and neat, rounded paws. Long, round-tipped tail. Broad, modified wedge-shaped head with medium–long, straight, large, wide-set ears. Large, almond-shaped, slightly slanted eyes.

Temperament

Very good-natured, friendly and affectionate. Adores being petted and played with and does not thrive if he lacks company (human or another pet). Good with children, dogs and other cats.

Colours

Currently all natural colours and patterns are allowed. Eyes can be blue, green, bright yellow to dark amber or odd-eyed.

Perfect owner

Someone with time to devote to this cat and plenty of inside space for him to run and jump in. If this is not available, a large secure outdoor pen should be provided so he can indulge in free energetic play.

Shorthaired

Safari Cat

affectionate • intelligent • athletic • alert • playful • energetic • gentle

SIZE medium to very large WEIGHT 2.5–11+ kg (5½–24+ lb) COAT close-lying, dense and soft
LIFESPAN 10+ years

The Safari Cat is a hybrid of the wild small South American Geoffroy's Cat (*Felis geoffroyi;* now an endangered species due to hunting for its fur) and domestic shorthairs. Breeders are few and far between, however, so there are not many Safaris available (in the USA only at the time of writing).

Behavioural characteristics
F1s and F2s can require a lot of attention. They have high energy levels and need plenty of space to run, leap and climb in order to keep them mentally and physically well. (A large secure outdoor run with play and climbing facilities is essential.) Later generations (F3s onwards) tend to be calmer.

Physical characteristics
F1 Safaris tend to be extremely large, while later generations are more normal in size.

Temperament
Breeders are striving to produce playful, gentle and loving cats.

Colours
Black with or without Black spots, Cream or Gold with Brown or Black spotting, Silver (the most typical); Calico, Torbie, Tortie and Orange are seen occasionally. Eyes usually yellow shades.

Perfect owner
A tolerant cat lover who appreciates the needs of these beautiful creatures (as far as F1s and F2s are concerned.) Having the right facilities to cater for their needs is all-important.

⚠ First- and second-generation (F1 and F2) cats need a high-quality commercial diet supplemented with raw and/or cooked meats, vitamins and extra calcium to cater for their 'wild' digestive tracts.

Shorthaired

Toyger California Toyger

loving • intelligent • active • alert • laid-back • sociable • friendly

SIZE **medium to large** WEIGHT **4–5.5 kg (9–12lb)** COAT **dense and soft** LIFESPAN **10+ years**

Shorthaired

The Toyger was developed by crossing Bengals with appropriately marked non-pedigree shorthairs in the late 1980s by Bengal breeder Judy Sugden in California. Her aim was to produce a cat that looked like a miniature tiger, and when she found a stray cat in India with the striped head markings she required to marry with her Bengals, she began her breeding programme with help from other enthusiasts. The breed is still under development today, with semi-longhairs cropping up, although the goal is for short, plush coats that stand away from the body for 'a bigger cat look'. It was recognized by The International Cat Association (TICA) in the early 1990s as a preliminary new breed.

Behavioural characteristics
Highly intelligent and resourceful. Enjoys running, climbing and leaping. Some lines are noisy at the moment. The breed's movement is purposeful, powerful and graceful.

Physical characteristics
Heavy-boned, rounded contours and muscular. Long body, tail and toes. Small, round ears. Straight, long, wide-ended nose with slight break. Large chin and square muzzle. Small to medium-sized, slightly hooded eyes.

Temperament
Affectionate and good-natured with people. Usually gets along well with children, dogs and other animals; at the moment, some lines are more sociable with other cats than others.

Colours
Tiger-like stripes in all ranges of Brown Mackerel Tabby, with a rufus colouring, dark stripes and white 'tiger' face, ear and underside colouring preferred. Eyes any colour except blue and pink (albino).

Perfect owner
Someone looking for an indoor cat, who can provide plenty of space for exercise and play.

Keuda American Keuda

energetic • agile • intelligent • affectionate • independent • playful

SIZE medium to large WEIGHT 4.5–7 kg (10–15½ lb) COAT close-lying, silky and shiny LIFESPAN 12+ years

Originating in Texas, the American Keuda is a breed that has naturally evolved. When Texan Jacque Brown and her college colleagues were conducting behavioural studies on colonies of farm cats on remote large ranches in the early 1980s, she became intrigued by this tactile breed. It was dubbed the Keuda – the acronym of the students' Kitten Evaluation Under Direct Assessment behavioural study program. Ms Brown picked out kittens that displayed the best qualities of the breed and embarked on a breeding programme to produce 'pretty, smart and tactile pets with a great personality'. The Keuda is still under development, but interest is increasing among breeders in the USA, and even Brazil.

Behavioural characteristics
Good hunter if given the chance. High energy levels. Will chat when spoken to, but not generally noisy. Loves to play with toys and will chase and may even retrieve them. Said to be inquisitive, outgoing and very determined to achieve his aim when he sets his mind to something.

Physical characteristics
Built for speed and agility, muscular, slim and strong. Distinctively, Keudas (like the Egyptian Mau) have skin flaps along the belly and behind the elbows to allow for ease of movement and to disperse body heat in hot weather. Very long guard hairs on the back.

Temperament
Loving and affectionate. 'Colony spirited', sociable with children, dogs and other cats. Dog-like in manner and personality. Adaptable to most environments.

Colours
All colours, but Blue, Black, White, Brown Tabby, Silver Tabby, Colourpoint and Smoke are preferred. Eyes deep gold in Blacks, blue in Colourpoints and Whites, and green in Blues and other colours.

Perfect owner
Someone who appreciates a pet with a big personality, and can provide plenty of safe room for him to run, climb and leap.

Shorthaired

Exotic Shorthair

affectionate • confident • friendly • gentle • playful • undemanding • dignified • placid

SIZE medium to large   WEIGHT 3–6 kg (6½–13 lb)   COAT dense, plush and soft   LIFESPAN 9+ years

Shorthaired

The act of crossing Persians with shorthaired cats, notably the American Shorthair, in a bid to improve Persian type and hardiness, produced what became known as the Exotic Shorthair. British Shorthair breeders also sought to improve their breed by doing the same. The breed's dense fur stands out from the body and benefits from a quick daily brush.

Behavioural characteristics
Laid-back, almost lazy, preferring to take life at a more serene pace than some of his more boisterous shorthaired counterparts. Playful and energetic when the mood takes him.

Physical characteristics
A Persian without the long coat, therefore nicknamed the 'Easycare Persian'. Cobby, large, rounded head and short, broad nose. Large, round eyes. Short, thick legs and big paws. Fur is longer than in other shorthairs, but not long enough to 'flow'. Some are more 'typey' (short-nosed) than others.

Temperament
Sweet-natured. Affectionate and gentle with all members of the family. They are confident cats, with the wonderful temperament of the Persian combined with the independence of the British and American Shorthairs. Does not mind being left on his own, and makes a good indoor pet.

Colours
Any of the many recognized British Shorthair or Persian colours, including Colourpoint, Tabby, Bi-colours, Selfs, Smokes, Pewter, Golden, Shaded and Tipped. Eye colours vary depending on the coat colour, but range from brilliant blue (in Whites) to copper (in Chocolates).

Perfect owner
Someone who would like a Persian but has little time or inclination for large amounts of daily grooming.

Kanaani Canaan Cat

affectionate • athletic • sociable • inquisitive • playful • hardy • adaptable

SIZE medium to large   WEIGHT 3.5–6.5 kg (9–14 lb)   COAT close-lying and fine; little undercoat

LIFESPAN 10+ years

Kanaanis were developed in the late 1980s/early 1990s by crossing non-pedigree, Oriental Shorthair, Abyssinian and Bengal. A handful of enthusiastic European breeders are presently working hard to develop and promote the breed and to increase its availability.

Behavioural characteristics
Self-assured, active and playful. Likes to climb and jump, so play facilities catering for these needs are essential. Good hunter and enjoys being outdoors given the opportunity, but also makes a fine indoor cat if he has the space to run about and toys to entertain him.

Physical characteristics
Large, lithe and muscular, with the slender look of an African wildcat. 'M' marking on the forehead.

Temperament
Good-natured and people-oriented. Curious and likes to be involved in whatever is going on in the house, but not overly demanding. Good with children, dogs and other cats.

Colours
Base coat colour ranges from ticked Yellow-Beige to Cinnamon. Minimum of three rings around the end of the tail. Spots are Seal Spotted Tabby (black pads and tail rings), Chocolate Spotted Tabby (chocolate pads and tail rings) or Cinnamon Spotted Tabby (brick-red pads and Cinnamon tail rings). Eyes gooseberry-, apple- or yellow-green.

Perfect owner
People who like an active and affectionate cat.

Shorthaired

Persian

easy-going • affectionate • devoted • undemanding • companiable • sociable • playful

SIZE **medium** WEIGHT **3–5.5 kg (6½–12 lb)** COAT **fine, long and thick** LIFESPAN **10+ years**

Longhaired

The ultimate – and true – longhaired cat, the Persian breed is hundreds of years old and is believed to have originated in Persia (now Iran). Since the beginning of the 20th century, enthusiasts have developed the type and extraordinary colour range that are seen today by outcrossing to other breeds (including Siamese). The original Persians had much longer noses than is fashionable nowadays.

Behavioural characteristics
Ideal indoor pets. Selfs tend to be very placid; Colourpoints are often livelier and more talkative. Home-loving, although some enjoy going outside and hunting.

Physical characteristics
Stocky, cobby, compact, short-legged.

Temperament
Even-tempered, gentle, affectionate and adores being petted. Good with children, dogs and other calm cats.

⚠ The coat will tangle and matt if not groomed daily (see pages 143–144).

Colours
Vast colour range in Self, Smoke, Shaded, Cameo, Shaded Cameo, Tipped Cameo, Pewter, Tabby, Tortie, Tortie and White, Bi-colour and Colourpoint. Eyes blue, copper, green, orange or odd-eyed, depending on the coat colour.

Perfect owner
Someone willing to spend lots of time each day grooming.

Variations

• **Colourpointed Persians** (with Siamese-style markings) are called Himalayans in the USA.
• **Kashmir** is a US term for Chocolate and Lilac Persians.
• **Himalayan Hybrids** is a US term for some self-coloured Self and Colourpoint crosses.
• **Peke-faced Persians** are those of ultra-type (short 'squashed' noses), and are prone to health problems.
• **Pixie Persians** are produced to be smaller than standard.

affectionate • playful • hardy • placid • quiet • alternately lazy and lively

SIZE **medium**   WEIGHT **2.5–5.5 kg (5½–12 lb)**   COAT **fine, silky, dense and long**   LIFESPAN **12+ years**

Chinchillas are the only Persians with green eyes. This spectacularly beautiful 'fairy tale' breed became famous when one of these cats appeared in James Bond films as the lap cat of arch-villain Blofeld. The breed originated in the 1890s, and is thought to be a result of crossing Silver Tabby and Blue longhairs, and was a particular favourite of Queen Victoria's granddaughter Princess Victoria. Chinchillas used to be considered more temperamental than Persians, but breeders have strived to correct this. They make ideal indoor pets.

Behavioural characteristics
Laid-back about everything, very lazy, prefers to snooze in a warm, comfortable place or on a lap to anything else, but does have bursts of activity and playfulness. Enjoys the occasional romp in the garden.

Physical characteristics
Cobby body with short, thick legs, but not as stocky as a Persian. Broad, round head with small ears set well apart, small and well furnished with fur. Snub nose (longer than most Persians).

Temperament
Generally very affectionate, quiet and placid, but can sometimes make his displeasure known by sulking and adopting a 'snooty' air.

Colours
Snow-white with black tipping on the guard hairs, which gives a 'sparkling' appearance. Nose should be 'brick-red' outlined in black. 'Kohl-lined' eyes emerald-green.

⚠ Requires grooming on a daily basis (see pages 143–144); otherwise his coat soon becomes matted.

Perfect owner
Someone who prefers a 'glamour puss' with 'sparkle', and is prepared for the great deal of grooming that is necessary.

Longhaired

Balinese

entertaining • fun-loving • intelligent • active • playful • talkative • affectionate

SIZE medium   WEIGHT 3–4 kg (6½–9 lb)   COAT flat-lying, fine and silky   LIFESPAN 12+ years

The Balinese is basically a Siamese with long hair and the same colour points. They were named Balinese by a breeder because they reminded her of Balinese dancers. The Javanese, as listed by a few cat organizations worldwide (but not the main ruling bodies), is the same as a Balinese but in non-Siamese recognized colours. Javanese are called Oriental Longhairs in the UK (formerly known as Angoras) and in some other countries, including the USA, and Mandarins in others.

Behavioural characteristics

Extremely agile and mischievous, gymnastic. Loves to play with toys and owners, and has a tendency to run up and down curtains while racing around the house. Enjoys exploring the great outdoors and climbing trees when given the opportunity, although makes a good indoor pet if he receives enough physical and mental stimulation.

Physical characteristics

Siamese conformation (see page 57) with long, plumed tail. Generally healthy and hardy.

Temperament

Generally excellent. Very adaptable to any home environment, and gets on with children, dogs and other cats. If there is no one in the house most of the time, consider a pair of kittens, so they provide company and entertainment for each other.

Colours

Colourpoints are Seal (and Tortie), Lilac (and Tortie), Blue (and Tortie), Chocolate (and Tortie), Caramel (and Tortie), Red, Cream, Apricot, Tabby and Tortie Tabby. Eyes bright, clear blue (the deeper the blue the better).

Perfect owner

Anyone who wants a chatty, amusing and affectionate companion who is never far from their side.

Birman

quiet-voiced • sociable • playful • home-loving • easy-going • affectionate
SIZE **medium** WEIGHT **2.5–6 kg (5½–13 lb)** COAT **silken, fluffy and luxurious** LIFESPAN **12+ years**

The 'Sacred Cat of Burma', legend has it, was born when an all-white cat stood guard over the body of a priest, killed by invaders in a Burmese temple. As he placed his paws on his dying master, the cat's yellow eyes turned sapphire blue and his legs turned brown – apart from his paws, which remained pure white.

In the real world, Birmans probably originated from crossing Siamese with Longhaired cats, most likely Persians or Longhaired Orientals, and it was in 1920s France that the breed was developed until they bred true to type.

Behavioural characteristics
People-orientated, loves company and does not mind dogs and other cats. Adores all who respect and treat him kindly. Generally not too bothered about going outside.

Physical characteristics
Long, stocky and muscular. Full ruff and slightly curly hair on stomach. Bushy, medium-length tail. Medium-sized ears set well apart. Medium-length nose with no 'break', just a slight dip in profile.

Temperament
Wants lots of attention and enjoys 'helping' with chores around the house. Has a gentle laid-back nature.

Colours
Kittens are born white but the colours develop at a few days old. Colourpoints are Solid, Tortie, Tabby and Tortie Tabby in colours that include Seal, Chocolate, Red and Lilac. Body colour varies but is always pale. Eyes sapphire-blue.

Perfect owner
Someone who appreciates this breed's quiet, gentle charm and requires a playful and affectionate companion, and is also prepared to perform the regular brushing and combing that this breed requires.

Semi-longhaired

⚠ Requires regular grooming (see pages 143–144).

Maine Coon

laid-back • lively • playful • sociable • friendly • affectionate • devoted

SIZE **medium to large** WEIGHT **3.5–8 kg (8–18 lb)** COAT **silky and weatherproof** LIFESPAN **9+ years**

Semi-longhaired

Originating in the state of Maine, North America (it is the official Maine State cat) hundreds of years ago, these gentle giants are thought to be derived from non-pedigree farm cats that became semi-feral.

A few rexed (wavy-/curly-coated) Maine Coons have appeared in litters in recent years and these are known as Maine Coon Rex or Maine Wave, but only in semi-longhairs. While some Maine Coon breeders are keen to develop this gene type, others wish to eliminate it. Only time will tell if it develops.

They are not noisy cats, but have a characteristic, and cute, 'chirrup' when communicating with their owners. Brush and comb weekly to keep the coat in good order.

Behavioural characteristics

Generally idle; prefers to laze, rather than run, about. Males tend to be 'dozier' than females. Not very inclined to climb. Prefers the chance to be allowed outside, even if only in a large enclosed pen with play facilities. Capable hunter and good with children, dogs and other cats.

Physical characteristics

Big-framed, solid, substantial, muscular body; his coat makes him appear even more massive. Large, tall ears with distinctive tufts on the tips. Large head and large, round eyes that are slightly slanted. Full-cheeked with a squared muzzle and long nose.

Temperament

Gregarious, playful, gentle and chatty. Loves to be cuddled and talked to.

Colours

All colours, except Chocolate and Lilac points and Colourpoint. Eyes green, gold or copper. Odd or blue eyes allowed in Whites.

Perfect owner

Someone with plenty of space, either in the country, where the cat will have the freedom to roam outside, or in a town, where the cat can live indoors (preferably with an outdoor pen).

Norwegian Forest Norsk Skaukatt/Norsk Skogkatt/'Wegie'

independent • self-assured • gentle • territorial • hardy • affectionate • outgoing

SIZE **large** WEIGHT **6–9 kg (13–20 lb)** COAT **long, smooth and shaggy; woolly undercoat**
LIFESPAN **10+ years**

One of the largest cat breeds, the beautiful Norwegian Forest, fondly known as 'Wegie', originated as an outdoor farm cat on Scandinavian farms hundreds of years ago. Wegies display remarkable similarities to the Maine Coon (see page 98). The breed featured at the foundation of Norway's oldest cat club in 1938. Norwegian Forests take up to 4 years to mature fully.

Behavioural characteristics
Thrives on outside freedom, but can be kept indoors when plenty of play and exercise facilities are provided. Sociable, but remains independent. Enjoys 'fishing' in shallow water, and is drawn to running water.

Physical characteristics
Massive and powerful, yet elegant. Long and muscular, but not cobby. In warmer countries, the weatherproof double coat is less thick in summer.

Temperament
Friendly, outgoing, alert and active. Not overly demanding. Gets on with children, dogs and other cats.

Colours
All colours and patterns allowed, although some countries (including the UK) disallow Chocolate, Lilac and Colourpoint (Himalayan). Any eye colour.

Perfect owner
A family with a garden and anyone prepared to spend time grooming.

Semi-longhaired

⚠ Requires regular grooming (see pages 143–144).

Siberian Siberian Forest Cat

agile • alert • hardy • fun-loving • intelligent • playful • devoted • inquisitive

SIZE medium to large   WEIGHT 3.5–6.5 kg (8–14 lb)   COAT thick, softly firm and glossy; dense soft undercoat
LIFESPAN 10+ years

Semi-longhaired

The Siberian's history dates back hundreds of years. Thousands of them are said to have been collected from different regions of the former Soviet Union following the siege of Leningrad (now St Petersburg) during the second world war to deal with the city's plague of rats, since the resident feline population had died or been eaten by starving inhabitants. Siberians arrived in the USA in 1990 and are now found in many European countries.

Their weatherproof fur can be slightly oily, which helps to keep dander (dead skin flakes) to a minimum, but regular brushing with grooming powder can help to remove excess natural oils from the coat, if necessary. They take up to 5 years to mature fully.

Colourpointed Siberians, which occurred naturally in the 1960s, are nicknamed 'Neva Masquerades'.

Behavioural characteristics

Great leaper and good hunter. Bold and hardy. Suited to living in very cold climates. Often wiggles his tail when happy. 'Chirrups' when talking, and purrs loudly.

Physical characteristics

Heavy-bodied, muscular, strong and sturdy. Long body and tail.

Temperament

Independent but very affectionate. Loves to play and interact with people. Good with children, dogs and other cats.

Colours

Almost any colour and pattern, with Brown Tabby being the most common. A white ruff and paws are common. Eyes any colour.

Perfect owner

Someone who can provide this cat with space to run and leap, and is prepared to brush and comb him regularly, even though he is said to require only minimal grooming.

Oriental Longhair

friendly • affectionate • home-loving • playful • sociable • extroverted • inquisitive

SIZE medium WEIGHT **3–4 kg (6½–9 lb)** COAT fine and silky LIFESPAN **12+ years**

Not to be confused with the Turkish Angora (known as simply the Angora in the USA), the Oriental Longhair used to be known in the UK as the Angora (or British Angora), and the Javanese or Mandarin in some countries. Its name was changed in the UK on 1 June 2003 to avoid misunderstanding.

Essentially, the Oriental Longhair is a longhaired version of the Oriental Shorthair, with both breeds being basically Siamese without the Siamese (Colourpoint) markings.

Oriental Longhairs originated in the UK in the early 1970s via the mating of Abyssinian (which carries a longhair gene) with Siamese. Further breeding with Siamese, Oriental Shorthair and Balinese created a large enough gene pool to maintain a set standard, but it took 30 years of selective breeding to achieve this.

Behavioural characteristics
Chatty and curious, likes to be involved in everything. Racing around the house one minute, curled up on your lap enjoying a cuddle the next.

Physical characteristics
Graceful despite solid build. Lithe and muscular, but svelte. Wedge-shaped head with large ears, and almond-shaped, slightly slanted eyes. Long, slim legs and small, oval paws. Plumed tail.

Temperament
Generally excellent.

Colours
Many: Selfs (including White and Red), Torties (including Blue and Fawn), Smokes, Shadeds, Tabbies and silvered colours. Eyes green except in Whites (blue or odd – one green and one blue).

Perfect owner
Someone who is willing to devote time and attention to this energetic cat, which needs company from either his owner or another pet (cat or dog).

Semi-longhaired

Ragdoll

easy-going • affectionate • loyal • vocal • fun-loving • sociable • gentle

SIZE **large** WEIGHT **4.5–9 kg (10–20 lb)** COAT **dense and silky** LIFESPAN **12+ years**

Semi-longhaired

So named because the original Californian breeder, Ann Baker, said they had a tendency to go limp when held, Ragdolls are one of the larger breeds of cat. They were developed by crossing a White Persian (or, as some say, an Angora) with a Birman in the early 1960s. Burmese were also introduced into the equation.

A popular myth is that Ragdolls are more impervious to pain than other cats. This not true. Nor is it true that their coats don't matt – they will if they are not groomed on a regular basis.

RagaMuffins are Ragdolls in a wider variety of colours than are officially accepted by major cat organizations, such as Van pattern, Smoke and Shaded Colourpoints. Cherubims, Honeybears and Miracle Ragdolls are all slight variations of the Ragdoll.

Behavioural characteristics
Docile, relaxed, playful and chatty. Prefers company, whether human, canine or feline.

Physical characteristics
Powerful and imposing, with long, muscular body, sturdy legs and large, round paws. Long, bushy tail. Eyes large, slightly slanted and oval.

Temperament
Sweet-natured, trusting and gentle. Good with children, dogs and cats.

Colours
Colourpoint (Solid, Tabby and Tortie in accepted colours), Mitted and Bi-colour. Eyes blue – preferably deep blue.

Perfect owner
An apartment dweller wanting an excellent indoor cat that thrives on affection and is devoted to his owner. He does enjoy going outside, but is safer enclosed in a spacious pen.

Turkish Van
Turkish Cat/Van Kedi

calm • easy-going • affectionate • playful • soft-voiced • home-loving • intelligent

SIZE **large** WEIGHT **4–8 kg (9–18 lb)** COAT **silky, crisply soft and flowing** LIFESPAN **12+years**

Turkish Vans originated in Turkey, unsurprisingly, hundreds of years ago. The cat matures fully at 3 years.

The all-white Turkish Van is highly prized in its native country, and was not introduced to the UK until the early 1990s. It is known as the Van Kedi (or White Van Kedi/White Turk) by some breed enthusiasts who are striving to have this colouring recognized under the name of Turkish Vankedisi. Blue-eyed whites are predisposed to deafness.

Behavioural characteristics
Most like playing with water. Curious, but content to watch the world from a windowsill.

Physical characteristics
Big, powerful and muscular, yet graceful.

Temperament
Well balanced. Affectionate and laid-back and prefers a relaxed, calm environment. Will not tolerate being over-enthusiastically manhandled by anyone. Sociable with dogs and other cats.

Colours
Chalk-white with colour markings on head (not below eyes and separated by a vertical white blaze), base of ears and tail. The best-known marking colour is Auburn, but most other natural solid, Tortie, Tabby and Torbie colours are accepted. Eye colours amber, blue or odd-eyed.

Perfect owner
Those who live a quiet life and require a loving, loyal and intelligent pet. He may be a bit clumsy, and will moult in clumps, so not ideal for the house-proud.

⚠ Care should be taken to run baths cold, before adding hot water, in case these cats get into the bathroom, jump into the water and scald themselves. It is also a good idea to keep toilet lids down.

Semi-longhaired

Turkish Angora Angora

elegant • graceful • quiet • home-loving • intelligent • playful • lively

SIZE small to medium   WEIGHT 2–4 kg (4½–9 lb)   COAT fine, silky and flowing   LIFESPAN 12+ years

Semi-longhaired

Like the Turkish Van, the Angora originated in Turkey, and is believed to have been introduced to the country centuries ago by Vikings. These cats are more finely built than Turkish Vans. It is possible, however, that they may be related to the Vans in the distant past. Zoos ensured the Angora's survival in the 1960s through a breeding programme, but bred only white cats. From there it was exported first to the USA, and later to other parts of Europe.

Today, Angoras are seen in all natural colours (Chocolate, Lilac and Himalayan pattern are not accepted). Some countries, including the UK, do not officially recognize the breed as regards showing status.

Behavioural characteristics
Loves climbing, running and leaping.

Physical characteristics
Described as 'long, slender and lightweight', although in reality quite solid. Long, full-brush tail often carried over the back, almost touching the ears.

Temperament
Generally excellent. Affectionate and sociable. Being more tolerant, the Angora is more of a child-orientated family cat than the Turkish Van – but this does not mean that he will put up with rough handling. Good with dogs and other cats.

Colours
Any colour except Chocolate, Lilac and Colourpoint. Eyes blue, shades of amber (from green to copper) or odd-coloured (blue and amber). Blue-eyed Whites are predisposed to deafness (as is true of the same colouring in other breeds).

Perfect owner
Someone who can provide peace and quiet, as well as plenty of space and facilities to indulge this cat's love of physical activity. Not suited to noisy households.

freedom-loving • agile • lively • playful • intelligent • active • companionable

SIZE **medium**   WEIGHT **3–5.5 kg (6½–12 lb)**   COAT **close-lying, soft and fine**   LIFESPAN **12+ years**

This breed is essentially a longhaired Abyssinian, albeit a bit bigger. It is unclear when and from what breeds the gene for long hair was introduced to this breed, but in the 1960s an American Abyssinian breeder was given a longhaired Abyssinian, and resolved to breed them under the name of Somali (the country bearing that name borders Ethiopia, formerly Abyssinia). Gradually, other breeders with longhaired Abyssinians helped to enlarge the gene pool.

There have been experimental crosses involving Somalis in an effort to create an 'all-white Somali' (the 'Suqutranese') and a heavy-boned silver breed (the 'Snow Cat/Alaskan Snow Cat'), but, at the time of writing, current breeding of these cats could not be confirmed.

The Abyssinian is an entertaining and independent companion that hates being kept inside permanently, unless there is plenty of room to run and play. Alternatively, outside freedom can be given in a large, secure pen with warm housing, space for running and facilities for climbing, jumping and hiding.

Behavioural characteristics
Extremely agile and athletic, incredible gymnast. Clever and resourceful. Prefers warmth.

Physical characteristics
Medium-long, muscular and lithe. Long legs and oval feet with tufted toes. Moderately wedge-shaped head with 'smiling' expression and wide-set, upright, long-tufted ears. Large, 'kohl-lined' eyes.

Temperament
Shy and reticent, but very affectionate with trusted people. Bonds strongly with owner.

Colours
Identical to the Abyssinian, with 28 colour variations in all (see page 56). Each hair has at least six bands of alternate base and ticking colour, which gives the breed's coat a breathtaking appearance. Eyes amber, hazel or green.

Perfect owner
An understanding person who is able to provide the necessary warmth, space and play facilities required by this breed.

Semi-longhaired

Nebelung Nibelung

intelligent • loving • devoted • laid-back • gentle • companiable • hardy

SIZE medium   WEIGHT 2.5–4 kg (5½–9 lb)   COAT two-layered, lustrous, fine and silky   LIFESPAN 10+ years

Semi-longhaired

The Nebelung (German for 'creature of the mist') looks like a longhaired Russian Blue and was founded by breeder Cora Cobb in the mid-1980s. The breed was developed from one blue semi-longhaired male kitten resulting from a mating between a black non-pedigree shorthair and a Russian Blue lookalike.

Another litter resulted, and this time Ms Cobb kept a blue semi-longhaired female. When they matured, the two siblings mated and the Nebelung resulted from Ms Cobb's following breeding programme, which included Russian Blues with recessive longhair genes and those with semi-long hair, including some from Russia.

The breed is still quite rare, but is increasing in popularity with breeders in the USA, the Netherlands, Russia and Germany.

Behavioural characteristics
Fairly laid-back and undemanding. Enjoys playing and climbing.

Physical characteristics
Long-bodied, medium-boned, sturdy, athletic, muscular and graceful. Long legs with oval, tufted paws, and long, plumed tail. Modified, long, wedge-shaped head with large ears and long, straight nose. Medium-sized, wide-set, slightly oval eyes.

Temperament
Gentle and affectionate, but shy with strangers. Dislikes noisy households and over-enthusiastic handling.

Colours
Blue tipped with silver. Eyes green.

Perfect owner
Those looking for a quiet, loving, non-demanding, preferably indoor pet, and who can provide plenty of space and facilities.

Tiffanie

affectionate • gentle • chatty • playful • intelligent • laid-back • home-loving

SIZE medium WEIGHT 3.5–4.5 kg (8–10 lb) COAT close-lying, glossy, fine and silky LIFESPAN 12+ years

The exceptionally pretty Tiffanie originated from the same breeding programme that created the Burmilla in the 1980s by crossing Burmese and Chinchillas. Some people refer to them as 'longhaired Burmese', which is not strictly true. The Tiffanie resulted from matings between Burmillas, when the longhair gene surfaced. This breed should not be confused with the Tiffany (Chantilly) (see page 108), which is of entirely different ancestry.

Behavioural characteristics

Particularly people-orientated and loves playing with his owner. Can be chatty, but not as vocal or noisy as his Burmese and Asian Self cousins. Laid-back and easy-going, he likes his home comforts, but occasionally will enjoy racing around. Clever and resourceful.

⚠️ Tiffanies require regular grooming to keep the coat tangle-free (see pages 143–144), but are nowhere near as labour-intensive as Persians and Chinchillas.

Physical characteristics

Solid and muscular, with conformation very similar to the Burmese (see page 62). Short, wedge-shaped head with large, wide-set ears that feature long inner hair ('streamers') and, sometimes, lynx-tufted tips. Large, wide-set, rounded, 'kohl-lined' eyes.

Temperament

Renowned for his wonderful friendliness and good nature. Good with children, dogs and other cats.

Colours

The wide range of colours is the same as for Asian Selfs (see page 58) and Burmese. Eyes are various shades of yellow through to green depending on the coat colour.

Perfect owner

A devoted family with plenty of play facilities and either indoor or secure outdoor space in which he can run, leap and climb.

Semi-longhaired

Tiffany Chantilly

affectionate • devoted • playful • companiable • sociable • gentle • intelligent

SIZE medium   WEIGHT **2.5–4.5 kg (5½–10 lb)**   COAT **close-lying, soft, smooth and silky**   LIFESPAN **10+ years**

Semi-longhaired

The Tiffany, or Chantilly, was developed in the USA in the late 1960s from a pair of golden-eyed, chocolate-coloured, longhaired cats of unknown breeding. The resulting kittens were registered with the ACA as Sable Foreign Longhairs.

The ACA dropped the breed when numbers failed to increase, and the breed almost became extinct, but enthusiasts embarked on a new breeding programme to preserve the Tiffany, which included outcrossing to Oriental Longhairs and Somalis, among other breeds.

While still rare outside the USA, the breed is slowly beginning to increase in popularity, thanks to its wonderful temperament and stunning good looks.

In 1992, the Tiffany's name was changed to Chantilly to avoid any confusion with the non-related Tiffanie (see page 107), but they are still referred to by many as the Tiffany or Tiffany-Chantilly.

Behavioural characteristics
Not too demanding or mischievous, and tends to bond closely with his owner. Soft-voiced chirps and trills form his vocabulary.

Physical characteristics
Elegant and graceful. Medium build with a medium-long nose and medium-sized ears that feature long 'streamers'. Plumed tail.

Temperament
Affectionate, loyal and devoted to his owner. Sociable and gets on well with children, dogs and other cats.

Colours
Rich Chocolate Brown (best known and most popular), Black, Cinnamon, Blue, Lilac and Fawn. Coat patterns include Mackerel Tabby, Ticked and Spotted. Eyes shades of gold.

Perfect owner
Someone who wants a loyal companion and who can provide a fairly quiet environment.

Cymric Longhaired Manx

laid-back • placid • intelligent • quiet • loyal • affectionate • courageous • strong

SIZE **medium** WEIGHT **3.5–5.5 (8–12 lb)** COAT **thick and fluffy double coat** LIFESPAN **10+ years**

While there had previously been some semi-longhairs in the breed, Persians were introduced into Manx breeding in the 1930s to improve coat quality and conformation.

There are several tail types: rumpy, stumpy and longie (see page 44 for details). While some cat organizations retain the name 'Cymric', others now class them simply as Longhaired Manx. The coat needs grooming once a week (see pages 143–144) to stop it becoming tangled. Cymrics take up to 5 years to mature fully.

Behavioural characteristics
Friendly and affectionate, likes being part of the family and is interested in everything that goes on. Protective of his home. Prefers a quiet, settled environment, but adapts when brought up in a busy household. Fierce hunter if given the opportunity, and excellent mouser. Likes to climb.

Physical characteristics
Most distinctively a lack of tail – ideally the rump should be completely rounded with no tail bone or cartilage to be felt. Solid and stocky body with a short back. Back legs longer than front, with powerful thighs. Round, large head with full cheeks. Broad, straight nose. Tall ears, set high on head and angled slightly outwards.

Temperament
Gentle and even-tempered. Amenable with dogs and other cats if brought up with them, but will soon 'see off' strangers.

Colours
All colours and patterns accepted; some cat associations will not accept Colourpoints (Himalayan pattern), Lavender and Chocolate, and the latter two colours with White. Eye colour should be in keeping with coat colour.

Perfect owner
Anyone prepared to wait for one of these rare cats will be handsomely rewarded with a loyal and devoted pet. Ideal for those wanting an independent but affectionate companion.

Semi-longhaired

York Chocolate

intelligent • loving • devoted • playful • energetic • calm • home-loving

SIZE **medium to large** WEIGHT **4–6 kg (9–13 lb)** COAT **soft and silky; no undercoat** LIFESPAN **12+ years**

Semi-longhaired

York Chocolates were developed in New York State in the 1980s from Chocolate-coloured, semi-longhaired farm cats. They are rare – there are only four breeders in the world (in the USA, Italy and France) – and are not widely recognized as yet, but demand for kittens is high owing to their beautiful appearance and colour, along with their suitability as family pets.

Behavioural characteristics
Adaptable to most environments. Loves to be held and cuddled. Enjoys interacting and playing with people. A great 'purrer', and said to have a fascination with water.

Physical characteristics
Muscular, sturdy, long body. Modified wedge-shaped head (longer than wide) with slightly concave, long nose and large, forward-pointing ears. Plumed tail and tufted paws. Medium-sized, almond-shaped eyes.

Temperament
Loves his owner passionately; very easy-going, calm and equable. Sociable with children, dogs and other cats.

Colours
Chocolate, Chocolate and White Parti-colour, Lavender, and Lavender and White Parti-colour. White only on the muzzle, nose, belly, legs and paws. Eyes gold, green or hazel.

Perfect owner
A family or individual wanting an affectionate yet playful pet as a devoted companion. If allowed outside, he should be kept in a large secure pen with play and climbing facilities for his own safety.

Non-pedigree Domestic/Moggy

playful • affectionate • agile • sociable • healthy • hardy • independent • territorial

SIZE small to large WEIGHT 1.5–5.5 kg (4–12 lb) COAT usually thick and close-lying LIFESPAN 12+ years

Known as the Domestic in some countries, the non-pedigree is of no definable breed or type. It occurs naturally without intervention by man, and has done for thousands of years, and belongs to the same species as the wildcat of Europe and Asia. The non-pedigree is the source, and mainstay in many cases, of all the pedigree breeds we know today.

Most non-pedigrees have short hair, since the shorthair gene is dominant, but coat textures, types and colours are widely varied, with many being Tabby – a colouring that harks back to wild ancestors.

The Romans are considered mainly responsible for the worldwide spread of cats after conquering Egypt.

Behavioural characteristics

Most non-pedigrees are good hunters and enjoy, even crave, the opportunity to go outside. Those not allowed to roam freely tend to be happy enough in a large pen that offers plenty of climbing, jumping and hiding facilities. They also like home comforts. Many are 'chatty' when talked to.

Physical characteristics

Shapes and sizes vary widely depending on ancestry. Generally very healthy and hardy.

Temperament

Generally excellent. Usually make devoted family pets.

Colours

Any. Self-Gingers (Reds) tend to be male, while Torties tend to be female. The most common colours are Tabby, Black (and White), Ginger (Red), and White (and other colours). Eyes of any colour.

Perfect owner

A family or individual wanting affection, companionship, devotion and entertainment in equal measures.

Short- & semi-longhaired

Scottish Fold

friendly • affectionate • playful • inquisitive • laid-back • gentle • sociable

SIZE **medium to large** WEIGHT **2.5–6 kg (5½–13 lb)** COAT **dense, soft and thick** LIFESPAN **10+ years**

Short- & semi-longhaired

The breed's unusual ears, which fold over to the front, are caused by a genetic mutation, which can result in skeletal abnormalities if two cats carrying the gene are mated together. Scottish Folds, therefore, are mated only to straight-eared cats and not back to Folds.

Kittens with normal ears born to Scottish Folds are known as Scottish Straights. Semi-longhairs are rare (caused by the Persian gene passed down from British Shorthairs) and examples are called the Scottish Fold Longhair (also known as the Highland Fold, Longhair Fold or Coupari).

The Foldex is said to be a cross between a Scottish Fold and an Exotic Shorthair, originating in Quebec, Canada. This is still at an experimental stage, and no further details were available at the time of writing.

Behavioural characteristics

Self-assured, quiet-voiced and loves to 'help' around the house. Not overly active and enjoys interactive play with owners.

Physical characteristics

Compact, powerful build with fairly short, stocky legs. Resembles the British Shorthair (see page 61) in coat type and conformation, apart from the folded ears, which can be tightly or loosely folded.

Temperament

Placid and sociable with children, dogs and other cats.

Colours

Any colour; Lilac, Chocolate and Colourpoint are not accepted by some organizations. Eyes any colour in keeping with the coat.

Perfect owner

Anyone who requires an interactive and affectionate pet. Working owners should consider getting two cats to keep each other company.

American Bobtail

sociable • loving • adaptable • loyal • talkative • agile • intelligent • gentle

SIZE medium to large   WEIGHT 3–7+ kg (6½–15½+ lb)   COAT soft thick topcoat; downy undercoat, dense, weather- and waterproof   LIFESPAN 12+ years

This all-American breed was developed some 40 years ago in Arizona when a bobtailed non-pedigree kitten was discovered. He was subsequently bred to a Siamese female. The resulting kittens eventually bred with other non-pedigrees, along with Colourpoint (Himalayan) Persians, with the short tails and unusual markings reappearing until a definite breed profile was produced. Bobtails take up to 3 years to mature fully.

Behavioural characteristics

Likes to climb and very outgoing. Quiet-voiced, but 'chirps, clicks and trills' when happy. Magpie-like, attracted to shiny objects.

Physical characteristics

Athletic, cobby, well-muscled and powerful. The naturally occurring bobbed 'powder-puff' tail, usually 2.5–10 cm (1–4 in) long, can be slightly curved and stands up when the cat is alert. Rolling gait. Eyes large, rounded, almond-shaped. Abundant inner ear hair and tufted ear tips.

⚠ The coat needs grooming every 2–3 days (see pages 143–144).

Temperament

Noted for dog-like personality and devotion to owners, said to get along well with children and other animals.

Colours

All coat colours and patterns acceptable. Eyes any colour.

Perfect owner

Someone who wants a friendly and affectionate pet that purrs a lot and likes to curl around their neck.

Short- & semi-longhaired

American Curl

affectionate • sociable • even-tempered • intelligent • quiet-voiced • curious • adaptable

SIZE **medium** WEIGHT **2.5–4.5 kg (5½–10 lb)** COAT **soft, silky and flat-lying; minimal undercoat** LIFESPAN **12+ yea**

Short- & semi-longhaired

The American Curl's curled-back ear tips are due to a gene mutation. Tufts of inner-ear hair further enhance and accentuate the ear shape. The incidence of curled-back ears was first seen in California in the 1980s. A curly-eared stray cat produced kittens with similarly curled ears, and a new breed was heralded.

The rexed-coat version (with the rex gene introduced from the American version of the Cornish Rex) of the American Curl is called the Ruffle.

Behavioural characteristics
Dog-like, tending to follow owner around, scared of missing anything interesting. Adjusts to home environments and other animals well, and remains happy and contented providing he receives enough attention. Retains a kitten-like character throughout life.

⚠ Care should be taken when handling the ear tips so as not to cause damage to the cartilage.

Physical characteristics
Moderately muscled and of medium bone and build. Medium-sized, modified wedge-shaped head with a medium-length nose. Tips of ears curve back in a smooth arch. Eyes large and round, walnut-shaped.

Temperament
Good-natured and likes lots of attention. Companionable and curious, likes 'helping' around the house, and trills and coos to talk.

Colours
All colours and patterns. Eyes can be any colour.

Perfect owner
An individual or family who will give their Curl an abundance of love and attention.

Japanese Bobtail

lively • sociable • friendly • intelligent • playful • talkative • energetic

SIZE **small to medium** WEIGHT **2.5–4 kg (5½–9 lb)** COAT **soft and silky; no undercoat** LIFESPAN **11+ years**

This unusual breed has been around for centuries in Japan, although it is still relatively rare outside its native country. Its distinctive short, curled tail is the result of a gene mutation, and when two 'Bobbies' are mated they will produce only Bobtails. In Japan, Bobtails are viewed in much the same way as non-pedigrees are in other countries, and there are few specific breeders, as the breed occurs naturally.

The Bobby's tail (known as a 'pom') is unique in that, while the short length and shape may vary, it is always curled, owing to its bends and kinks. As the tail vertebrae are often fused together, the tail should never be forcibly straightened, otherwise the cat will suffer great discomfort.

Behavioural characteristics

Happy to be inside or outside, where he likes to play and climb, given the opportunity. Generally hardy and healthy with no problems.

Physical characteristics

Hind legs noticeably longer than forelegs. Large, round eyes slant upwards. Tail always short and curled (from behind, the Bobby looks almost like a rabbit).

Temperament

Sweet-natured and sociable with humans, dogs and other cats. Loves to be cuddled and enjoys playing with his owner.

Colours

Any colour except Silver, Ticked Tabby and Colourpoint. Most popular is 'Mi-Ke' (Japanese for 'three colour': Tortie and White, comprising red, black and white). Eyes any colour, with odd eyes particularly prized.

Perfect owner

A person or family requiring an affectionate, talkative house cat.

Short- & semi-longhaired

Kurilian Bobtail

devoted • agile • athletic • affectionate • calm • tolerant • hardy

SIZE **medium to large**   WEIGHT **4–10 kg (9–22 lb)**   COAT **fine and dense**   LIFESPAN **12+ years**

Kurilian Bobtails have been known about since the second half of the 20th century, when Russian military people and scientists brought these cats back with them from the mainly uninhabited Kuril Islands (located between Russia and Japan).

Kurilian Bobtails are rare outside their native islands and Russia, but there are some breeders in Europe and the USA. The natural, wildcat appearance belies the Kurilian's docile and charming personality.

Behavioural characteristics
Excellent hunter and likes playing with water. Agile and athletic; likes to climb and enjoys being outdoors given the opportunity.

Physical characteristics
Compact and powerful. Short kinked or curved 'pom-pom' tail.

Temperament
Affectionate and good with children, dogs and other cats, although male Bobtails (entires and neuters alike) are said not to tolerate other male cats, as they are very competitive.

Colours
Any colour except Colourpoint, Chocolate, Cinnamon, Fawn and Lilac, and these colours combined with White. Agouti is favoured. Eyes yellow to green; Whites, Vans and Harlequins can have blue or odd eyes.

Perfect owner
A family with or without outdoor facilities. If kept indoors, he must have plenty of space and facilities for mental and physical exercise.

LaPerm Dalles LaPerm/Alpaca Cat

affectionate • gentle • sociable • inquisitive • playful • hardy • adaptable

SIZE small to medium   WEIGHT 2–4.5 kg (4½–10 lb)   COAT soft, wavy/curly; no undercoat   LIFESPAN 12+ years

An American breed, the LaPerm originated in 1982, when one non-pedigree barn cat produced a hairless kitten that developed a curly coat as it grew older. This kitten in turn produced both curly- and straight-haired kittens. This bunch of barn cats inbred and created more and more curly-coated cats, until this became the norm instead of the exception among them. The LaPerm coat is caused by a dominant rex gene.

LaPerm breeders use the terms BC (born curly), BS (born straight) and BB (born bald) as part of their kittens' pedigree names, as this helps them to track the curly coat gene.

Behavioural characteristics
Curious by nature. Generally quiet, but can be talkative. Enjoys being outdoors given the opportunity, but also makes a fine indoor cat because of his strong owner-bonding instinct.

Physical characteristics
Looks delicate, but lithe, well-muscled and 'foreign' in appearance. Bottlebrush tail in shorthairs; curly, plumed tail and ruff in semi-longhairs. Coat length and thickness varies and coats can be wavy through to tightly ringleted. Long curly whiskers. Eyes large, almond-shaped and slanted.

Temperament
Very affectionate, adores being cuddled. Sociable with dogs and other cats. Playful and 'kittenish'.

Colours
Any coat and eye colour (including odd eyes).

Perfect owner
People who want a loving companion with a big personality.

Short- & semi-longhaired

Pixie-Bob

intelligent • sociable • friendly • exuberant • adaptable • quiet • confident

SIZE **medium to large** WEIGHT **3.5–9 kg (8–20 lb)** COAT **weatherproof, semi-dense and soft** LIFESPAN **10+ years**

Short- & semi-longhaired

Cats of Pixie-Bob type are believed to be centuries old, as wild bobcats began breeding with domesticated cats brought to North America by settlers. In 1985, some enthusiasts started a breeding programme with these cross-breeds to develop a cat with a naturally wild appearance but a gentle temperament. Carol Ann Brewer is the breeder accredited with first producing the Pixie-Bob. They take up to 4 years to mature fully.

Behavioural characteristics

Inquisitive and displays unusual behaviour, such as burying food, stealing and collecting small, preferably shiny, items. Likes playing with water. Chirps and chortles when chatting to owner.

Physical characteristics

Looks similar to the wild American bobcat, but smaller. Muscular and rangy, with heavy bone structure, loose skin and large feet (often with extra toes, as polydactyl paws are a feature of the breed; up to seven toes are acceptable). Naturally short tail, hence the name.

Temperament

Dog-like devotion to his owner. Gentle, and good with children, dogs and other cats. Bonds strongly with his family.

Colours

Only Brown Spotted Tabby is accepted for showing, but other colour variations of this are being bred, including rufous shades of Russet, Fawn and Tan with brown to black markings with white ticking. Eyes gold to brown; gooseberry-green accepted.

Perfect owner

A family or individual looking for an indoor pet, providing there is plenty of space for exercise and play. This cat needs lots of mental stimulation.

Selkirk Rex

affectionate • quiet • patient • playful • sociable • calm • tolerant

SIZE **medium to large** WEIGHT **3–5.5 kg (6½–12 lb)** COAT **soft, dense and curly** LIFESPAN **10+ years**

The Selkirk Rex originated in the USA in 1987. Jeri Newman, a Montana cat breeder, developed the breed from a curly-/short-haired non-pedigree female kitten and a Black Persian. Jeri embarked on a breeding programme for her Selkirk Rex, as she named her new breed, which included outcrossing to Persian, British Shorthairs and Exotic Shorthairs to produce the type that prevails today.

The so-called Missouri Rex (a curly, medium- to long-coated non-pedigree/Devon Rex cross), found in the mid-1980s, was genetically tested and found to have the same 'curly' gene as the Selkirk Rex.

Behavioural characteristics

A mix of all the breeds that were used in its development – British Shorthair calm and reserve combined with Persian/ Exotic Shorthair playfulness and affection.

Physical characteristics

Sturdy, muscular, cobby build similar to a Persian. Heavy-boned. Round head with large, round eyes. Tightness of coat curls or ringlets varies depending on coat length, but generally loose and wavy. Curly whiskers and eyebrows. Plumy tail and ruff in semi-longhairs.

Temperament

Loving and loyal. Even-tempered and good with children, dogs and other cats.

Colours

Any coat and eye colours.

Perfect owner

A super companion for someone prepared to spend time grooming.

⚠ Requires regular grooming (see pages 143–144).

Short- & semi-longhaired

Munchkin

playful • affectionate • sociable • friendly • intelligent • outgoing • inquisitive

SIZE **small** WEIGHT **1.5–3.5 kg (3½–8 lb)** COAT **short: plush but not thick; semi-long: silky** LIFESPAN **10+ years**

Short- & semi-longhaired

Munchkins are basically cats with little legs. There is no difference between them and non-pedigrees, apart from the fact that they have noticeably shorter limbs owing to a genetic mutation that affects the long bones of the legs.

Since the breed's introduction into the public eye in Canada and the USA in the 1980s, over 30 spontaneous occurrences of Munchkins have been reported; the dwarf gene appears sometimes to occur spontaneously even in pedigree cats. They are named after the little people in the film *The Wizard of Oz*.

Behavioural characteristics
Often steals and hides objects that take his interest. To get a better view of the world around him, he sometimes perches on his haunches and sits up. A proficient hunter.

Physical characteristics
Variable appearance like the non-pedigree, but short-legged. Agile and quick, very much like a squirrel. Generally healthy and hardy.

Temperament
Sweet-natured, generally getting along well with children, dogs and other cats. Self-assured with a cheerful personality.

Colours
Any coat and eye colour. Semi-longhairs are not as prolific as the shorthair varieties.

Perfect owner
City apartment dwellers and those who live and travel in recreational vehicles, who want an indoor cat; when outside, he must be penned for safety.

Variations
Munchkins crossed with Persians and Munchkins crossed with Exotic Shorthairs are called **Napoleons**; they are essentially short-legged Persians and Exotic Shorthairs.

Skookum

playful • agile • curious • friendly • affectionate • intelligent • sociable

SIZE small   WEIGHT 2.5–3.5 kg (5½–8 lb)   COAT semi-long: soft; short: wiry   LIFESPAN 10+ years

A Skookum is a cross between a LaPerm and a Munchkin. The breed originated in the USA when some LaPerm breeders, who also bred Munchkins, decided to try a hybrid cross in the late 1980s and early 1990s. The idea was to produce a short-legged cat with curly hair, although this does not always happen as, at the time of writing, the breed is still too new for a standard to have been set.

To date, due to their varied genetic mixture, mating two Skookums can produce a mixed litter of LaPerms, Munchkins, Skookums and non-standard kittens (those that have neither a curly coat nor short legs).

> ⚠ Great care should be taken when socializing both Munchkins and Skookums, as the breeds are too small to cope with unfriendly actions or behaviour from other pets.

Behavioural characteristics
Said to be 'cute like the Munchkin and bright like the LaPerm'. Agile and quick-moving. Can jump and leap like his longer-legged relations, but not with the same range.

Physical characteristics
Around 15 cm (6 in) high at the shoulder, Skookums have a similar conformation to the Munchkin, with a body in proportion set on short legs, with rather large, rounded paws. Large, almond-shaped eyes.

Temperament
Lively and sociable. Gets on well with anyone, as well as dogs and other cats.

Colours
Any colour coat, including Colourpoint, and eyes.

Perfect owner
Almost any household wanting a friendly and endearing feline companion. Perfect indoor cat – or may be allowed outside in a secure large pen.

Short- & semi-longhaired

Desert Lynx

active • energetic • patient • tolerant • affectionate • outgoing • sociable

SIZE medium to large WEIGHT 3.5–9+ kg (8–20+ lb) COAT silky and soft; thick undercoat LIFESPAN 10+ years

The Desert Lynx is a cross between the wild bobcat (*Felis rufus*; North American Lynx with a barred and spotted coat and short tail) and a variety of both short- and bobtailed and short and semi-/longhaired domestic breeds (including Pixie-Bobs, Manx and American Bobtails) to produce a wild-looking bobtailed 'designer' hybrid. The breed standard states that the Desert Lynx should not contain less than 12.5 per cent bobcat blood.

Where and when they were first bred is unclear, but they have increased in popularity in recent years, although breeders are few and apparently only in the USA at the time of writing.

Behavioural characteristics
Active and energetic, loves to climb, run and leap. 'Dog-like' personality. Alert, intelligent and resourceful.

Physical characteristics
Strong and muscular. Bob or short tail. Individuals sometimes feature six toes on all four feet (polydactyl).

Temperament
Friendly and outgoing with people he knows. Playful and enjoys interacting with his owner, but not 'needy'. Good with children, dogs and other cats.

Colours
Sorrel, Ebony, Chocolate, Fawn, Silver, Snow, Bronze and Blue. Patterns are Clouded Leopard (Marbled Tabby), Tawny (Ticked Agouti) and Leopard Spotted (Spotted Tabby). Eyes blue in Snows and yellow-green in other colours.

Perfect owner
Anyone wanting a striking and companiable family pet, and who can provide plenty of space for exercise and play.

Short- & semi-longhaired

Highland Lynx

sociable • laid-back • affectionate • outgoing • playful • sociable • active

SIZE **large** WEIGHT **6–9 kg (13–20 lb)** COAT **medium-hard to soft; thick undercoat** LIFESPAN **10+ years**

The Highland Lynx breed was founded in the USA in 1995 by crossing Desert Lynx (see page 122) for conformation with Jungle Curls (comprising wild Jungle Cat [*Felis chaus*] x Hemingway Curl [curled-ear domestics] x other domestic breeds) to introduce curled ears.

A fully domesticated cat with the look of the North American Bobcat (*Felis rufus*, also known as Red Lynx or North American Lynx, which should not be confused with the larger Canadian Lynx, *Felis canadensis*), the Highland Lynx is slowly gaining in popularity. These cats will adapt to most environments given time and patience. Breeders are few, however, and only in the USA and Puerto Rico at the time of writing.

Behavioural characteristics
Active and energetic, but not overly so. Enjoys running, climbing and jumping. 'Dog-like', intelligent and resourceful. Usually not vocal.

Physical characteristics
Strong and muscular with a stocky body, chunky legs and large, tufted paws. Tail varies in short length from no tail to halfway to the ground. Individuals sometimes feature six toes on all four feet (polydactyl).

Temperament
Affectionate and outgoing with known people. Playful and enjoys interacting with his owner. Good with children, dogs and other cats.

Colours
Sorrel, Ebony, Chocolate, Fawn, Lilac, Silver, Mink, Snow, Sepia Brown and Blue. Patterns are Tawny (Ticked Agouti), Leopard Spotted (Spotted Tabby) and Clouded Leopard (Marbled Tabby). Eyes blue in Snows, and shades of gold through to green in other colours.

Perfect owner
A family or individual with indoor and outdoor secure pen space to cater for the Highland Lynx's size and exercise needs.

Short- & semi-longhaired

American Ringtail Ringtailed Sing-a-Ling

happy • confident • playful • agile • chatty • athletic • affectionate

SIZE medium to large WEIGHT 3.5–5.5 (8–12 lb) COAT soft and velvety double coat LIFESPAN expected to be 10+ years

Short- & semi-longhaired

Originally known as the Ringtailed Sing-a-Ling, the American Ringtail was renamed in June 2004. The breed was founded in 1999 in California. The cats were so named because they 'ring' the tail (carry it up and over their backs like Husky dogs) when happy and confident; this is due to a naturally occurring gene mutation in shorthaired non-pedigrees (domestic cats), from which the new breed is derived. Breeders are outcrossing to the Ocicat and also intend to outcross to Ragdolls and to Russian Blues.

Ringtails can be bred to Ringtails without any detrimental effects, which is not the case with some other mutated breeds.

Behavioural characteristics
Chatty, playful and engaging. Chirps and miaows often, but not loudly. Natural athlete that enjoys testing his agility. Big personality and very alert. Adaptable.

Physical characteristics
Tail carried over the back and to the side in a flexible curl. Muscular and lithe. Large, round and expressive eyes.

Temperament
Friendly and outgoing. Gentle, sweet-natured and people-orientated. Good with children, dogs and other cats.

Colours
Any colour coat. Eyes – blue is expected for Colourpoint cats, and ranging from green through to copper for other colours.

Perfect owner
A family or person looking for an active and curious cat that will interact with them a lot and is great with children.

Sphynx Canadian Sphynx/Canadian Hairless/Moon Cat/Temple Cat

outgoing • affectionate • inquisitive • mischievous • playful • intelligent • energetic

SIZE **medium** WEIGHT **3–4 kg (6½–9 lb)** COAT **none (feels like suede)** LIFESPAN **10+ years**

While there have been reports of hairless cats from early in the last century, it was not until the 1960s that the Sphynx originated in Canada, comprising the foundation stock for all Sphynx today. Devon Rex and American Shorthairs were used in the early developmental stages to expand the gene pool and set a type. The lack of hair is caused by a mutated, recessive gene.

The Sphynx needs more food than other cats in order to generate sufficient energy to keep warm and to move around energetically. Kittens' eyes open early, even from the day they are born.

Behavioural characteristics
Very 'purry'. Drawn to warm places due to lack of insulating fur.

Physical characteristics
Fine-boned but muscular and sturdy. Long, whippy tail. Wrinkled scalp.

Temperament
Gentle, patient and sociable. Good with children, dogs and other cats.

Colours
Any colour skin and eyes.

Perfect owner
A devoted cat lover looking for an indoor cat, and who can provide the care and attention the Sphynx needs.

⚠ Sphynx cats are susceptible to cold, so they must have a warm environment. Lacking protective fur, they are prone to skin injuries. They require wiping over, particularly in between the wrinkles, with a soft damp cloth, plus the occasional bath when necessary, to remove oil and dirt from the skin, and must be dried thoroughly. Ears and nails may also require regular cleaning to remove waxy deposits.

Hairless

Don Sphynx Don Hairless/Don Bald Cat/Donsky/Hairless Russian Cat

friendly • sociable • intelligent • affectionate • active • energetic • athletic

SIZE small to medium WEIGHT 2.5–5.5 kg (5½–12 lb) COAT 3 types: nude (suede-like), velour (flock-like) and brush (fine and wiry) LIFESPAN 10+ years

Hairless

Both of the new Russian hairless cat breeds, the Don Sphynx and Peterbald (see page 127), were founded in 1988 with the discovery of a hairless female in Rostov-on-Don. The cat was passed as healthy by veterinary experts, and was mated to a European Shorthair (see page 83) in 1989 and produced hairless kittens, which in turn produced more of the same when mated to European Shorthairs; the new breed was named the Don Sphynx.

Some of these foundation Don Sphynx stock went to St Petersburg, where they were mated with Oriental Shorthairs and Siamese and, in 1994, produced hairless kittens of Oriental type that were dubbed the Peterbald (Petersburg Sphynx). Genetically, both types are unrelated to the better-known Sphynx (see page 125).

They are rare outside Russia, with only a few in other countries, including the USA – although they are growing in popularity. Kittens open their eyes extremely early, or may be born with opened eyes, which can cause problems.

Behavioural characteristics
Having no fur coat for insulation, he is drawn to warm places. Very devoted to his owner and loves to be cuddled.

Physical characteristics
Resembles a bald European Shorthair. Normal teeth and claws. Females have a musky odour. Thick, curly whiskers (if any).

Temperament
Very friendly, almost dog-like in his response to humans.

Colours
All skin pigments (or hair colour when present) acceptable, from solid colours to Torties and Tabbies. Eyes any colour.

Perfect owner
Someone wanting an indoor cat who is prepared to provide extremely careful management as, being hairless, the Don Sphynx has no natural protection against cold and wet weather and is prone to injuries.

Peterbald Don Hairless/Hairless Russian Cat/Petersburg Sphynx

friendly • sociable • intelligent • affectionate • active • energetic • athletic

SIZE **small to medium** WEIGHT **2.5–5.5 kg (5½–12 lb)** COAT **3 types: nude (suede-like), velour (flock-like) and brush (fine and wiry)** LIFESPAN **10+ years**

See Don Sphynx (page 126). The gene responsible for hairlessness in the Peterbald and Don Sphynx is a dominant one, so only one copy of it is sufficient to produce hairless kittens, whereas in the Sphynx the hairless gene is recessive, meaning that two copies of it are required to produce nude cats (both parents must carry it).

Behavioural characteristics
Seeks out warm places to sit and sleep, as susceptible to cold. Demands physical contact from humans. Very 'touchy-feely' – he will reach out to pat his owner's face gently with his paws. Lively.

⚠ Must be kept indoors, and may need a cat coat in cold weather.

Physical characteristics
Resembles a bald Oriental Shorthair and is described by breeders as 'elf-like'. Sturdy, lean and graceful. Longer, finer-boned body than Don Sphynx, with more wedge-shaped head. Eyes are small and oval.

Temperament
Extremely friendly and attention-seeking, sociable. Good with children, dogs and other cats if brought up with them.

Colours
Any colour acceptable, including Colourpoint. Eyes green-gold, but blue in Colourpointed cats.

Perfect owner
A person prepared to provide careful management, for the same reasons as for the Don Sphynx. Suitable only as an indoor cat, as he needs to be kept warm and dry.

Hairless

CARING FOR YOUR CAT

You can start caring for your cat even before you collect him by being well prepared to welcome him into his new home. If you have all the equipment needed to keep him happy and healthy, and understand how to introduce him to the family and other pets and how to look after him correctly, you will make his experience of settling into his new home far less stressful.

Many rewards

Caring for a cat is immensely rewarding. He is relying on you for so many things – feeding him the food he likes, keeping his litter tray clean and giving him a helping hand in keeping his coat in tiptop condition. He will then reward you when you least expect it by responding to his name for the first time, or by suddenly jumping on to your lap for a cuddle. During this early time you will learn about your cat's 'personality', his likes and dislikes, his favourite toys and places to sleep, and when he wants to have time alone.

Getting off to a good start

This section describes all you need to know about caring for your new pet. Many people assume that because cats are so independent there is little work involved in looking after them. However, despite their self-contained nature, cats can be quite time consuming and need as much care and attention as any other pet.

Starting with travelling home safely and first introductions, there is lots of advice on how to ensure that your cat has the best start for his new life.

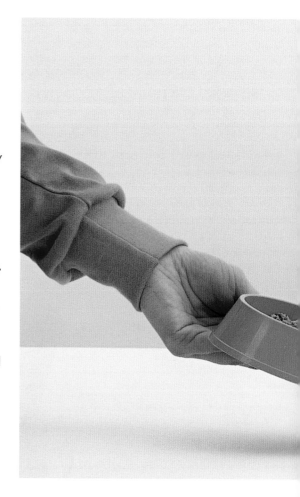

Begin by being prepared: buy everything you will need in advance, including bed, litter tray, toys and scratch post, and you can then concentrate on his welfare once he arrives home. There are tips on how to introduce him to the rest of the family and to resident pets as well as advice on litter training, handling and how to interact with your new cat. Once he's settled, it will be time to make some decisions: will he be an indoor or outdoor cat? Should he wear a collar and/or be microchipped? A responsible owner will consider every option.

Be prepared to welcome your new cat to his home with some good food.

Caring for your cat

Being prepared

You will need to make sure that everything is ready to welcome your new cat into your home. Being properly prepared will make the first few days less stressful for both you and your cat. There are lots of different pet products in the shops, so look around to find the ones you think will be most suitable for your cat.

Essential equipment

Make a list of the equipment you will need before the arrival of your new cat:

- Carrier
- Litter tray
- Litter
- Scoop
- Food
- Food bowl
- Water bowl
- Feeding mat
- Grooming kit
- Scratch post
- Toys
- Bed
- Collar and identity tag
- First-aid kit (see page 187)
- Cat pen
- Parasite treatment

Place his litter tray, bed, food and water bowls, toys and scratch post in the room in which he will be confined for the first few days.

Cat bed

There are dozens of different kinds of cat beds now available to suit every kind of home. A traditional wicker basket with a cushion is ideal, or you could choose a cushion-type bed, either in a doughnut shape or hooded, which provides an element of privacy. A cardboard box is the cheapest type of bed, but make sure it is well padded with cushions or blankets. For older cats, there are now special types of bedding that reflect the cat's body heat, helping to keep him warm. Cats also love beds that hook on to radiators and act like a cradle or hammock.

There are many different cat beds available, in various shapes and sizes.

messes over the edge; this is not deliberate – simply an indication that you need a larger tray. A covered tray is ideal for an adult cat. It prevents litter being sprayed around the floor and helps to contain the smell, as well as offering the cat privacy.

Litter

Cats can be quite fussy about the type of litter they prefer, but generally fuller's earth (clay) clumping litter is best. This litter absorbs moisture and forms a clump that can be easily lifted out, leaving the clean litter behind. It is relatively inexpensive, but heavy to carry. There are many other types of litter, including pellets (made from recycled materials such as paper) or silica sand crystals.

It's essential to have a litter tray and litter ready for the arrival of your new cat.

Place the bed somewhere quiet where your cat won't be disturbed. He will want to see it as a place of sanctuary, and if he is constantly disturbed he will seek somewhere else to sleep. Many owners complain that their cat refuses to sleep in the beautiful, expensive bed they have bought. But while you may see it as the most comfortable cat bed in the world, cats are fussy creatures and if he prefers to sleep on a pile of ironing you won't be able to persuade him otherwise.

Whichever type of bed you choose, remember that it should be cleaned regularly. Bedding should be washed to remove dirt, and sprayed with a household flea treatment to prevent flea infestation.

Litter tray

If you are getting a kitten, you will need to provide a litter tray with low sides that his short legs can easily climb over. Later you can change this to a more permanent tray. The litter tray should be large enough for the cat to be able to squat comfortably to relieve himself. If it is too small, you may well find that he

Caring for your cat

Caring for your cat

Toys

Cats love to play, so ensure you have plenty of toys to entertain your cat, particularly for the first few weeks when he will be kept inside. Table-tennis balls and soft toys filled with catnip are great favourites. Fishing-rod toys, which comprise a stick and elastic with a toy on the end, are perfect for interactive play, but you should never leave a cat alone with this toy (or any other toys with elastic attached) because he can get the elastic tangled around his neck.

Scratch post

Your cat will need a scratch post on which to 'strop' his claws (see page 144), especially if you want to deter him from using your furniture for this job. Ideally, the sisal-covered post should be high enough for the cat to reach up with his fore legs to strop. Multi-level activity centres are ideal since they offer cats the opportunity to jump and scratch as well as a high place to sleep. Some cats like to strop their claws by reaching forwards with their forelegs and will use the carpet for this. Scratch posts that lie flat on the ground will suit these cats.

Microchipping

Microchipping is a permanent method of cat identification. A microchip the size of a grain of rice is painlessly inserted via a needle into the thick skin at the back of the neck. Each microchip contains a number which corresponds to a number on a central database where the contact details of the owner are held. Any lost cat taken to a vet or rescue centre is scanned with a handheld scanner to see if he has been microchipped. If he has, the scanner will detect the microchip and the number will be displayed on the scanner. The vet will then contact the database to get the owner's details.

Collar and identity tag

Your cat may already have been microchipped before you collect him (see box). However, you may decide you want to put a visible form of identification on your cat too. A collar and identity tag will allow people to see

immediately that he is not a stray, and, if he gets lost, to return him to you quickly. You can also attach a bell to the collar to prevent your cat from catching birds and small mammals (the bell will warn the prey of the cat's presence, though see page 157).

However, you must be careful regarding what type of collar you buy. Safety collars are designed to open quickly if the cat gets the collar snagged on a branch or other object. Always test the product in the shop to see how easily it opens before purchasing one. Don't buy collars that have a buckle with a prong that fits into a hole. You should be able to fit two fingers between the cat's neck and the collar. Check this regularly, particularly on growing kittens. If you choose to use a flea collar on your cat, don't use other flea treatments at the same time or you will overdose your cat on the chemicals they contain.

Bringing your cat home

Make sure you are completely prepared, and have allowed time to welcome your cat to his new home. It is a good idea to plan to have at least a couple of days at home to keep him company and to offer reassurance during his settling-in period. He will need plenty of peace and quiet during this time.

Collecting your cat

If you are able, take the bedding your cat is to use, or one of your old jumpers, to the breeder's house or to the rescue centre a few days before you collect him. This will serve two purposes: first, he will get to know your smell, so when he arrives home he will recognize your

Collecting your new cat is an exciting time for all the family.

scent in his new surroundings; second, it will transfer his smell to the bedding, making him feel more at home in his new house. Also, if you are able, ask for some used litter from the breeder. This can be added to his new litter tray, again familiarizing the cat with his new home.

It is a very exciting time and it is easy to forget vital details, so if you are buying a pedigree cat make a list of what to get from the breeder, including a receipt for the purchase, pedigree papers, registration forms and vaccination certificates. Rescue centres will also provide the relevant paperwork.

Cat carrier

You must have a suitable carrier in which to transport your cat. Check that the one you buy has the following:

- Enough space for the cat to be able to lie down and turn around inside the carrier.
- A secure fastening – ensure that the opening can be fastened securely and that the cat cannot undo the catch. Remember, cats are Houdinis in disguise.
- Strong material – a terrified cat can rip its way through cardboard, so don't use an ordinary

Ensure you have a suitable basket or carrier so your cat can travel safely. A wire cat carrier is ideal.

cardboard box. Instead, buy a plastic or wire carrier, or a strong cardboard carrier designed for the purpose.

- Plenty of ventilation to keep the cat cool and for air.
- A solid waterproof base – the cat may urinate through fear, so line the base with newspaper, with a towel placed on top, to absorb the wet.
- A strong handle that won't break.

When you put the cat in the carrier, try to be as calm as possible. Cats are highly sensitive to human emotions and will sense any anxiety you are feeling.

On the road

If you are driving your cat home, secure the carrier on the back seat with the seat belt so that it won't move if you have to stop quickly. There is no need to put any

food inside the carrier, as the cat will be too stressed to want to eat. Take water to give to the cat if you are travelling a long way and make stops so he can drink. Don't travel on a hot day unless you have air-conditioning in your car; a frightened cat will quickly become dehydrated. Though you may think the journey will be short, you should allow for traffic delays or the car breaking down. Don't drive too fast, and take corners gently; your cat won't like being flung around inside his carrier. Cats have extremely sensitive hearing, so don't play loud music in the car. Instead, talk to the cat so that he gets to know your voice and is reassured.

Some cats become extremely distressed when travelling in a car. Your vet may prescribe a mild sedative for future long-distance journeys, such as moving house.

Top tip

Never allow a cat to travel free in a car. He can distract the driver and cause an accident, or even jump through an open window. Many cats will appear to be very distressed in a car, but ignore their frantic miaowing. Just talk gently to the cat to calm him. As soon as the cat is taken out of the car, he will stop his protesting and you will realize that he is fine.

Confinement

It's essential that you confine your new pet to one room for the first few days. He will be disorientated and anxious, so keeping him in one small area will help to make him feel more secure, particularly if he has been living in a pen at a rescue centre.

Prepare the room in advance by placing his litter tray in one corner and his bed and food bowls in another area. The stress of the journey may have dehydrated him so make sure there is water for him to drink.

Once you arrive home, place the carrier in a quiet room where there are no other pets. Open the carrier door and then sit quietly on a chair and wait for the cat to leave the carrier. He will first want to smell his new environment and may take some time to emerge.

Your new cat should be confined for the first few days to allow him to get used to the new smells of the house. He is also much less likely to escape. Keep the windows and door shut and, if necessary, put a note on the door to remind the family to be careful when going in and out.

> ⚠ Remember to open doors slowly – the cat may be just behind the door and could be seriously injured if it hits him.

Settling in

Remember that your cat will need time to adjust to his new surroundings, so don't hurry him: give him time alone to sleep and regain his energy. After a couple of days, introduce him to the rest of the house. After he has been allowed to explore other rooms, always return him to his own room, where he will feel safe and be able to relax.

After a few days, you can leave the door of the room open and allow him to wander at his leisure around the house (first checking that all the windows are closed). At this stage you can move his bed, food and water bowls and litter tray to their permanent position in the house and show your cat where they are. Kittens may forget and need to be taken to their litter tray to relieve themselves for the first few times. Don't shout at or hit your cat or kitten if he refuses to use his litter tray. A new environment is unsettling for cats and anxiety can lead to toileting problems (see pages 167–168).

Don't allow your cat to go outside the minute you get home or he may wander off and get lost.

Top tip

Keep the bed, food and water bowls separate from his toilet area. Cats are very clean animals and will not eat or sleep near their litter tray.

Making introductions

It is vital that initial introductions are carried out properly, as they can make or break relationships in the house. Encourage each member of the family to spend time in the room with the new cat. Explain to everyone that he will be frightened and may hide but given time he will come out to explore his new home.

Making friends

By sitting still in a chair and ignoring him, you are showing the cat that you are not a threat. When he comes up to you, don't attempt to touch him – just talk quietly without looking at him. People who dislike cats often complain that they are the one a cat will immediately approach. This is because such people tend not to look at the cat, which for the cat is a clear sign of friendship and a non-hostile gesture. For cats, staring is a sign of aggression, so by closing your eyes or looking in a different direction you are indicating that you are a friend and wish to avoid confrontation.

Once he is comfortable around you, you can start to stroke him and eventually pick him up. Of course, this process will be considerably shorter for kittens or very outgoing cats. Kittens are much more inquisitive and less fearful of humans. They also need to be rescued from trouble, so early handling is inevitable.

It can take minutes, hours or even days for the cat to come out of hiding. An outgoing, well-socialized cat will be curious to see who you are. A timid cat may spend days hiding under furniture, creeping out a little at a time and watching you. Be patient and don't try to catch him; eventually he will learn that you are a friend and not a threat and will come to you of his own accord. Cats are curious creatures and, as long as he feels safe, he will want to explore his new environment.

Children

Children will be very excited at the arrival of their new pet, but it is essential that they are kept calm and quiet. Don't allow very young children to handle kittens without supervision, as they can easily hurt them. Older children should understand that they can handle their new pet only for short periods until he has grown used to them. Explain that it is far better to spend time quietly ignoring the cat because this is a sign of friendship.

Explain to children how to watch the cat for signs that he is angry or annoyed so they can avoid being scratched. A kitten won't inflict much pain with his tiny claws, but an older cat will protect himself if he feels threatened, and his sharp claws will hurt. Read the section on behaviour problems (pages 159 and 170–171) to recognize the signs of an unhappy cat and know how to deal with them.

Always supervise young children. They may be too rough with kittens, or be scratched by an older cat.

Animal introductions

It is vital that resident pets and the new cat are carefully introduced or they may never bond. A cat pen is especially useful (see page 21) because it both protects the new cat and prevents him from running away and hiding. Animals rely on scent to give them information about friends and foes, so start by transferring the smell of the existing pets to the new cat, and vice versa. Stroke the resident pet, then immediately stroke the new cat, then return to the resident pet. You could also use two cloths: wipe each animal with one of the cloths and then leave it in the other animal's bed. This scent transference will prepare the way for face-to-face introductions.

Other cats

After a couple of days of scent transference, place both cats in the same room, preferably at feeding time so that their attention will be distracted by food. If you have a cat pen, feed the new cat in his pen. If you don't have a pen, place the food bowls some distance apart and keep a careful eye on the two cats. Hissing and spitting is a natural part of introducing two cats, but separate them, if it's safe to do so, if they fight.

Introducing the new arrival to the resident cat will need careful supervision. Be prepared for hissing and spitting while the cats establish a pecking order.

Dogs

A dog's instinct is to chase, while a cat's instinct is to run. It is vital to prevent this happening when a dog and cat first meet or you will set up an unbreakable cycle. Keep the dog on a short lead and take him into the room, preferably with the cat in a pen. The dog will be very inquisitive and want to smell the new arrival. Allow him to sniff but not to get too close to the cat: a swift smack with extended claws can leave the dog with a nasty scratch. If you don't have a cat pen, hold the cat so he can't run away, but don't allow the dog too close. Once they have spent some time smelling one

another, keep hold of the dog but allow the cat to jump down and hide. Eventually the dog will grow bored with this uninteresting house guest and lose interest.

This process will probably need to be repeated several times, always with the dog on a lead so he cannot chase or frighten the cat. Initially, the cat will hide, but with persistence the cat should learn that the dog is not a threat, while the dog will learn that the cat is part of

Cats and dogs can be friends, but it takes time for them to learn to trust one another.

the 'pack' and won't chase him. Never leave a dog and cat alone in a room until you are sure they are happy and safe in one another's company.

Other pets

If you have small animals, such as mice or hamsters, be very careful. After all, it is a cat's instinct to hunt and kill rodents, and they can be very clever and persistent when they see prey. A strong cat can push the average hamster cage off a table. Make sure the cage is secure, or keep the cat out of the room. Remember to cover fishtanks to protect the fish.

Routine care

Your cat is an independent character and he will enjoy exploring his new home and territory, but it is your responsibility to keep him safe and healthy. By learning how to care for your cat and providing him with good food, regular grooming and plenty of love, you will be giving him the best home possible.

Food and water

It is essential that you provide the same type of food the cat is used to. A sudden change in diet can cause stomach upsets, so ask the breeder or rescue centre what kind of food he has been fed. You can change his diet later on, but do so gradually, first mixing a small amount of the new food into his bowl then increasing it gradually until it makes up his entire diet.

Don't worry if the cat refuses to eat initially. Settling into a new home can be a stressful time. However, if you are concerned, take your cat to the vet to be checked.

Make sure your cat has access to a bowl of water at all times (see page 178). For more information on feeding, see pages 176–177.

Litter training

You may want your cat to relieve himself outside, but while he is confined he will need a litter tray inside the house. Check what type of litter the cat has been used to and continue to use the same type. Remember the following tips:

Providing regular meals in a clean bowl is an important part of caring for your cat.

- Don't site the litter tray near feeding areas. Cats are clean animals and may refuse to use the litter tray.
- Remove dirty litter every day and clean the tray thoroughly at least once a week.
- Ideally, there should be one litter tray for each cat in the household.
- If your cat refuses to use the tray, try moving it to a more private spot.

Once the cat is allowed outside, start to mix soil into the litter in his litter tray, gradually increasing the amount. This will help him to associate toilet activity with soil. After a few days, move the litter tray outside, on to the

Top tip

Remember that kittens can have accidents. Never shout at or hit a kitten for relieving himself in the wrong place; he won't understand and as a reaction he may toilet behind furniture, where it is less obvious. After the kitten has eaten, pick him up and place him on the litter tray.

area where you want him to relieve himself, and show him where it is. Finally, remove the litter tray and mix a small amount of used litter into the area so that he will associate the smell with toilet activity. If you rake the soil into a fine tilth, it will encourage him to use that area (cats prefer an easy life and won't dig compacted soil).

Grooming

Cats are extremely clean creatures and groom themselves to remove dirt and hair, but this loose hair is swallowed and in large amounts can lead to furballs (see pages 184–185). By grooming your cat, you will help to prevent furballs. This is particularly important during the summer months, when animals moult and lose large amounts of hair.

Grooming is also essential for longhaired cats to remove mats and knots. The grooming process is made much easier if the cat becomes used to being groomed while he is still a young kitten. For his first grooming sessions, use a baby's brush-and-comb set; these are soft and won't hurt the kitten, who will learn that grooming can be a pleasurable time spent with his owner. If you are buying a pedigree kitten, ask the breeder for advice on how to groom the coat.

Grooming once a week is enough for a shorthaired cat, but longhaired cats need thorough grooming daily. When choosing a cat, you must bear this in mind, and ask yourself if you will have the time to devote to daily grooming if you get a longhaired cat.

Equipment

- **Soft brush**, for brushing the coat.
- **Rubber grooming brush** – massages the skin and removes loose hair.
- **Wide-toothed comb**, for teasing out knots.
- **Slicker brush** – a wire brush that penetrates the coat to remove loose hair.

Longhaired cats must be groomed on a daily basis. Ask the breeder to show you the best way to groom your cat.

- First gently brush the cat all over.
- Next use a comb to tease out knots.
- Finally give a thorough brush with the slicker brush.

Ensure that all areas of the cat are groomed. On longhaired cats, pay particular attention to between the hind legs. This is a very sensitive area, so be gentle and don't tug at knots.

Stropping

When you see your cat frantically clawing at the carpet or the sofa, he is not being deliberately destructive. He is actually 'stropping' his claws, which is a means of removing the old sheath from the outside of the claws to expose the new, sharp claw underneath. Each time he starts to claw at the carpet or walls, carry him to his scratch post.

Handling your cat

Interaction is an important part of the socialization process for kittens and for bonding with an adult cat.

Sleeping

Cats will sleep for up to 16 hours a day, so don't be alarmed if your new cat seems to spend large amounts of time in bed. Kittens will sleep for up to 20 hours a day.

⚠ Never pick up a cat by the scruff of his neck. Though cats pick up their young in this way, the kitten is so light that he is not harmed by it. Once a cat is older, the weight of his body can cause damage to the ligaments and muscles in his neck.

Support your cat by placing one hand under his hindquarters and the other under the chest. Hold him firmly but not too tightly.

Lifting and holding a cat

It is important to lift a cat safely. Sit on a chair and lift the cat on to your lap; the cat will have something to sit on and is closer to the floor for him to jump down if he wants to. Always use two hands, one under the chest and the other under the hindquarters. Hold him firmly but not too tightly or he may panic and struggle to escape. Keeping him close to your body will make him feel safe. Lift and hold your cat for only a short time, and always put him down if he struggles. By putting him down before he escapes you are teaching him that you are in control of the situation.

Remember that allowing himself to be picked up shows a huge amount of trust on the part of your cat. It is unnatural for a cat not to have the option to escape, and having all four paws removed from the ground makes him feel vulnerable. Some cats never enjoy being picked up, so if your cat struggles, don't persist. Always handle your cat gently and watch to see how he is reacting.

Touching and stroking

The head, face and paws are highly sensitive areas of the body, so touch these areas gently and stop if the cat's pupils enlarge or his body tenses. Cats often love to be stroked at the base of the tail and will lift their bottom upwards. Many people find this an odd movement, but it mimics the action of a kitten when he offers his bottom to his mother to be cleaned, and is a sign of trust.

Health and safety

Cats are perfectly capable of taking care of themselves, but there are many hazards in a house and it is your responsibility to ensure that his new home is a safe place for him to live in. If you think that your cat is sick or injured, take him to the vet. Check the health section (pages 174–193) for signs of ill health.

Indoor safety

It is almost impossible to anticipate what a cat will do, but by taking precautions you can do your best to ensure your cat is safe in his new home. You may think that your cat is perfectly safe indoors, but this is far from true.

Washing machines and tumble dryers

Cats are attracted to open washing machines and tumble dryers because they are cosy places to sleep. *Always* check that your cat is not inside before turning on either of these appliances.

Fridges and freezers

The smell of food lures cats to investigate fridges, while a curious cat may climb inside an open freezer. Check before closing the door that your cat has not sneaked in.

Cookers and hobs

A cat will jump up on to work surfaces to investigate smells, and could burn himself on a hot hob or cooker. If your hob or cooker does not have a heatproof cover, shut your cat out of the kitchen until it has cooled down.

Electrical leads

Kittens in particular love to chew flexes and leads, which can prove fatal. Make sure these are tidied out of the way, and check them regularly for signs of chewing.

Needles and thread

Sewing materials are extremely hazardous to cats. Needles can get stuck in the throat, while thread can become tangled in the gut, proving fatal. Keep needles, thread, buttons and elastic bands away from your cat.

Cleaning fluids

Household cleaning fluids should always be put away with the lid screwed on tightly. Mop up spills immediately.

Plastic bags and strips

Keep plastic bags in a cupboard, and always cut up the plastic strips that hold cans of beer together. A kitten can push his head through the plastic and be strangled as he struggles to free himself.

Powder carpet fresheners

The powder in these products can cause irritation to your cat's skin and paws, as well as respiratory problems, so avoid using them.

Human medicines

Store these carefully where your cat will not have access to them, and never give human medicines to a cat.

Hot water

Keep your cat out of the bathroom while you are running a bath as he may jump up to investigate and fall into the scalding water. Alternatively, run the cold water first to prevent such an accident.

Indoor plants

Some indoor plants are highly poisonous to cats, who may be tempted to nibble the leaves while they are housebound and don't have access to the outside. Keep these out of the way of your cat. You can buy 'cat grass' from your local pet shop for your cat to eat.

Windows

Close windows in upstairs rooms while your cat is being kept inside. He may try to escape, even through a small window, and fall. Although a cat can

Remove house plants to prevent your cat nibbling the leaves and provide 'cat grass' while he is confined to the house.

right himself to land on his paws, falling from a upper-storey window can cause serious damage, particularly if he lands on concrete. Alternatively, nail some netting over the window to prevent your cat jumping through.

Doors

It can be easy to forget that your cat may be right behind you as you walk through the house. Never slam doors or you may catch his tail. Don't open doors too quickly, either, particularly if you have a kitten: your cat may be on the other side and unable to react quickly enough to get out of the way.

Kittens

Kittens are small and often hide behind cushions on sofas. Before you collapse on to a chair for a rest, check that the kitten is not about to be squashed!

Caring for your cat

Outdoor safety

Once your cat is allowed outside, he will have the freedom to roam as he wishes, but you can still help to minimize the dangers he will face.

Garages/sheds

Always close garage and shed doors securely, checking that your cat is not shut inside. Hazardous materials stored in a garage or garden shed can kill a cat.

Cars

Cats like to sleep under cars, so check before driving away that your cat has not taken refuge underneath. In winter, cats may climb under the bonnet from beneath the car for warmth, so it is worth checking that your cat is not hiding in there before you turn on the engine.

Plants

There are many garden plants that are poisonous to cats, but they usually know instinctively which ones to avoid eating. Kittens, however, are less discriminating, so keep an eye on your kitten while he is outside.

Trees

Cats love climbing trees because it gives them a good vantage point. It is very rare that a cat will actually become 'stuck' in a tree. Usually, he will find a way down eventually, particularly if 'smelly' food, such as fish, is left at the foot of the trunk.

A cat is rarely truly stuck in a tree and will find a way down if left to his own devices.

Ponds and water butts

Keep a lid on your water butt. A cat that falls in has no way of climbing out again, and may drown. Ponds with steeply sloping sides are equally dangerous, especially if they contain fish, which will attract a cat. Create steps or a slope so that if your cat falls in he can climb out again.

Cats at night

There are several reasons why it is important to keep your cat in during the night, both for his protection and to preserve wildlife.

A cat's favourite times are dawn and dusk, when small rodents and birds are active. To stop your cat hunting, keep him inside during these periods.

More cats than ever are being killed on the roads, particularly at night when drivers simply don't see the cat in time to stop.

Cats are more likely to be stolen at night, even by 'pranksters' who find it amusing to take a cat in a car, and then let him out a long way from home.

⚠ Anti-freeze is lethal to cats, who find the sweet taste attractive. Even a small amount can kill a cat, so always lock anti-freeze in a cupboard and immediately clean up any that has been spilt.

When cats go missing

A missing cat is a very stressful experience and can lead to heartache if he is never found. Cats who are allowed outside are most at risk, but indoor cats can escape too. This is what you should do if your cat goes missing.

- Search the house thoroughly, and then search it all over again.
- Check wardrobes, boxes and drawers, and the loft space if you have recently been in there.
- Look in fridges, freezers, washing machines and tumble dryers, as well as the airing cupboard.
- Check high-up places such as on top of wardrobes and bookcases. Look inside your shed, garage and the car.
- Check your dustbin – food smells may have attracted him to climb inside.
- Ask your neighbours to check their garages and sheds as well as their dustbins.
- If there are skips in the area, search them: old carpets and sofas make ideal places for a sleep.
- If you can't find your cat, put 'lost' notices in local shops and contact your local vets and rescue centres.
- Make 'missing cat' leaflets to put through neighbours' doors or to attach to treetrunks or lamp posts, providing it is legal in your area to do so.
- Put a notice in your local newspaper's 'lost and found' column, and check there to see if your cat has been found.
- There are several 'lost and found' sites on the internet, so it may be worth checking these.

Caring for your cat

Indoors or outdoors?

Many cats, particularly pedigrees, are now kept as indoor cats – they are never allowed outside. Others have access to an outdoor run, or are confined to an enclosed garden. But many owners prefer to allow their pet the freedom to roam, and to come and go as they please. Here are the pros and cons for keeping your cat in or letting him out.

Enclosing your garden

Enclosing the garden, or building a cat run in your garden, is a good way to give your cat the best of both worlds. He is safe from dangers such as roads and thieves, but can enjoy fresh air, climbing and playing on grass. You will also avoid possible confrontations with neighbours who may object to your cat using their garden as a toilet, or 'fishing' from their pond.

An outdoor run allows a cat to enjoy fresh air but ensures he is safe from harm.

Access to the outside world

The longer you keep your cat inside the more likely he is to recognize and accept his new home. Keep him in for at least 2 weeks, preferably longer. A kitten will need to be kept inside until he is vaccinated. Don't allow a kitten out until he is at least 3 months old, and then monitor him in the garden; don't allow him to explore further as he is at risk of being bullied by older cats. A female kitten can become pregnant when she is as young as 4 months old, so keep an eye on her while she is outside until she has been spayed.

Leads

Many cats can be taught to walk on a harness and lead, in much the same way as a dog. This allows indoor cats the opportunity to explore outside without the danger of escape. Getting a kitten used to a harness at a young age will make training your cat much easier. Always train your cat inside the house where he will feel safe and secure.

Put the harness on your kitten and let him get used to the feel of it. Once he is happy to wear the harness,

INDOORS AND OUTDOORS: PROS AND CONS

Type of cat	Advantages	Disadvantages
Indoor cat	• He is safe from busy roads • Prevents theft of pedigree cats • His health is easily monitored • You always have your companion cat with you • He can't stray	• He may suffer from behavioural problems caused by boredom or overcrowding • He will be more prone to obesity • He may become frustrated if he has previously been allowed outside • It is not a natural existence for a cat
Outdoor cat	• He can live a more natural life, hunting and enjoying fresh air and exercise • He is less likely to become overweight • He is less likely to suffer from behavioural problems associated with boredom	• He will be more prone to parasites such as fleas, ticks and worms • He is more likely to be knocked down on the road • He may be stolen or mistaken for a stray • He may be injured in fights with other cats • He may go missing • If a female cat is allowed outside before she is neutered, she may become pregnant

clip on the lead and hold it lightly (don't put any pressure on the lead) and let him wander around. If he shows any distress, calmly take the lead off again. Keep training periods short, increasing the amount of time as your cat gets used to the feel of the harness.

Once he is perfectly happy to wear the harness and lead, take him in the garden to explore. Note that it can take weeks or months to lead-train your cat.

Pedigree cats are now usually prevented from roaming free to protect them from theft or injury.

Caring for your cat

Care while you are away

Cats prefer to stay in their own home while their owners are away, so ask family, a friend or a neighbour to look after your cat. Alternatively you can hire the services of a pet sitter who will either visit your house every day to feed your cat, or will live in to take care of your pet in your absence. The other option is to take your cat to a cattery.

Catteries

Choosing a good cattery is essential for both the welfare of your cat and your own peace of mind. Visit the cattery to satisfy yourself that it is suitable for your cat. If you have never used a cattery, ask a friend to go with you for support and write down a list of questions you want to ask. Here are some points to check:

- The cattery owner should make you feel welcome and be happy for you to inspect the premises, as well as be willing to answer any questions you may have. All catteries are licensed by the local authority, so ask to see the licence.
- Everything should be scrupulously clean, including the cubicles, food bowls and litter trays, and there should not be a smell, either of dirty litter or of too much disinfectant.
- The pen should have plenty of light and fresh air, with an enclosed area that is warm and dry. There should be room for your cat's bed, a scratch post and a window where your cat can sun himself. See if the resident cats seem happy and relaxed.
- Is there a kennels attached to the cattery and, if so, are the cats disturbed by the proximity of the dogs?

- Heating, preferably thermostatically controlled infra-red heaters, should be installed in each pen, but you should not have to pay extra for this. There should also be an enclosed outside run.
- 'Sneeze barriers' should be installed between pens. These are solid partitions that prevent infection from other cats.
- Pens should have double doors that prevent cats from escaping.
- Ask to see the food preparation area. This should be a separate room with food and medication clearly labelled for each cat.
- The cattery owner should ask about your cat's history and note what food your cat requires, any medication he needs and your contact details, as well as those of your vet. Avoid any cattery that does not ask to see your cat's vaccination certificates.
- Cats can and do become ill while in a cattery, so check what procedure is followed if there is an emergency.
- Finally, observe how the cattery owner interacts with cats: do they show a genuine love of cats? Though one cattery might be clean and well run, if you are not satisfied that the owner has the cats' interests at heart, it won't be the right place for your cat. Ask to speak to any staff who are employed to care for the cats.

Well-run catteries are very popular so book well in advance to ensure a place for your cat.

Going to a cattery for the first time can be a daunting experience for a cat, so start by booking him in for an overnight stay. Do this several times, so that he gets used to the cattery and being away from home. When the time comes for him to stay for a week or two, your cat will be able to settle in quickly. Your cat should be allowed to take his own bed and favourite toys, which will help him to feel more at home. It is also a good idea to leave an item of your clothing with him, but *don't* wash the clothing first as it is your smell he needs as a 'comfort' blanket.

Cats can be safely left in a cattery for several weeks. Prices vary, though a more expensive cattery is not necessarily better than one that charges less. Note that popular catteries are often booked up months in advance, particularly at peak holiday times.

BEHAVIOUR

Once your new cat is settled, and your house has become his home, you will realize that there is far more to cats than you had ever imagined. There is a reason for everything a cat does, no matter how inexplicable it is to his owner. In this section, you will learn the secrets of your cat's behaviour, and what happens when he is unhappy in his home.

Origins and evolution

It is believed that cats are descended from a weasel-like creature called a miacid, which lived around 60 million years ago. Around 2.5 million years ago, 40 species of wildcat, descended from the miacid, survived the Ice Age and developed into the wildcats of Europe and Asia. These animals had the skills needed to be super-efficient hunters, ensuring their survival over millennia. It was this skill that first drew the cat to the attention of humans 4,000 years ago. Today, many of its behavioural traits remain unchanged, simply because these assets continue to make the cat an extremely successful species.

Domestication

Although cats may have been domesticated elsewhere, almost all evidence points to Ancient Egypt as the place where, around 4,000 years ago, cats were first taken into homes as pets. Their primary purpose was to protect precious grain stores from rats and mice, and they became highly prized commodities. Wall paintings show that cats also performed other tasks for their masters, including accompanying them on hunting expeditions to flush birds from cover. The importance of

Cats have been domesticated for thousands of years and were used by hunters to flush birds from cover.

Behaviour

cats in everyday life saw them elevated from workers to pets and then worshipped as gods. From 1580 BC, a cat cult associated with Bast, the goddess of fertility and motherhood, developed.

Yet it was not only in Egypt that people recognized the importance of cats. Another cat deity, called Li Shou, was worshipped by farmers in China, because of the cat's importance in protecting crops from rats. In Norway, a pagan cult worshipped Freya, the goddess of love and fecundity, who was strongly associated with cats. Through his hugely successful rodent-control role, the cat soon became an essential worker on farms around the world.

Their supreme hunting skills made cats indispensable, and they have been worshipped as gods and goddesses all over the world, from Egypt to China and Norway.

High value

In Wales, Hwyel the Good, a prince of southern Wales, instigated a law in AD 936 that decreed that a kitten was worth one legal penny until he had opened his eyes, twopence until he was capable of killing mice and fourpence once he had reached hunting age. This made the theft or slaughter of a cat an extremely serious offence, and resulted in heavy fines to be paid to the owner.

Hunting

Although hunting is instinctive to cats, the techniques needed to become an accomplished hunter are honed in kittenhood in the form of play, and therefore kittens who are isolated from other cats tend to be poor hunters. Using toys to play with a kitten will help him to develop these skills. Cats invariably slow down as they get older, catching fewer prey and showing less enthusiasm.

Hunting habits

Some cats are more prolific hunters than others and may become frustrated if deprived of the opportunity to hunt. This may develop into unprovoked attacks on other targets, including people and other pets (see page 170).

It is a fallacy that starving a cat will make him a better hunter. Instead, a well-fed cat will have the energy to catch more prey, though his lack of appetite means that he will tend not to eat what he has caught.

Cats will catch rodents such as mice, voles and shrews, and birds. Though some cats do catch rats, a large rat is a fearsome opponent for all but the most accomplished of hunters. Some cats confine their hunting to non-edible prey, bringing in worms, toads and frogs, while others hunt larger prey including rabbits and large birds such as pigeons.

Bringing home 'presents'

Cats will return to their home carrying prey, either alive or dead. It is not entirely understood why they do this, but it is generally believed that the cat is bringing fresh

Cats are instinctive hunters and will often return home with a 'present' for their owner.

food home for his owner, whom he considers to be a poor hunter. This altruistic behaviour is also seen in feral cat colonies, where hunters will return to share prey with other cats in their social group.

You may find that your cat will drop the prey and then roll on his back to receive attention as a reward for bringing food. If the animal is still alive, you may be able to catch it and return it outside, though generally the shock will kill small rodents. Though owners can be greatly distressed by this, there is no way of deterring a

Playing with prey

Cats will often 'play' with their prey before finishing it off. For large prey, repeated shaking and pouncing is a means of forcing it into submission, whereas playing with smaller prey may be a means of perfecting hunting techniques.

hunting cat from bringing in prey. Attaching a bell to the collar of your cat may help to warn prey of his approach, so giving it the chance to run away, though many cats can move without shaking the bell.

Common behaviour patterns

Apart from hunting, cats exhibit a number of common types of behaviour, some of which are difficult for owners to cope with. Learning about the sounds your cat makes, his body language and behaviour will help you to understand how your cat is communicating, which will make owning a cat a more pleasurable and fulfilling experience.

Body language

How we wish our cats could tell us what they want. What most of us don't realize, however, is that they do! Cats use their entire bodies, as well as sounds, to convey a wide range of feelings from contentment to fear, from anger to friendship. Look for the signs in the chart opposite to see what your cat is saying to you.

Purring

It is still not known definitely how cats purr. Although it seems to come from the cat's throat, some scientists believe that the noise is caused by blood flowing from the heart through the liver and diaphragm, setting up vibrations in the sinus cavities of the skull. However, most experts agree that purring is produced by the vibration of the false vocal cords – membranes that are located near to the vocal cords.

Mother cats purr to let their kittens know they are near, and kittens begin to purr at just 1 week old. Young cats purr in a monotone, while older cats have two or three tones. Cats also purr at different volumes: some purr very loudly, while to hear others purring you may have

Spending time with a contented, purring cat is one of the best aspects of cat ownership.

to put your ear against their flank. All cats purr at the same frequency, however, which is around 25 cycles per second.

INTERPRETING YOUR CAT'S BODY LANGUAGE

Part of body	State	Meaning
Tail	Relaxed	Cat is content
	Held stiffly upwards	Sign of greeting, friendliness
	Held stiffly outwards	Intense concentration (when hunting)
	Held downwards and curled under	Cat is frightened or anxious
Eye pupils	Widely dilated	Fear, surprise or anger
	Narrow	Cat is relaxed and friendly
Ears	Erect	Cat is alert but friendly
	Held back	Fear or anger
	Flat on the head	Cat is very angry or fearful

Behaviour

Purring indicates that a cat is content and relaxed, but a cat will also purr when he's in pain. In both cases, the purr may be a submissive gesture to indicate he is unwilling or unable to defend himself.

Mewing or miaowing

Kittens mew to indicate to their mother that they are cold or hungry. Later this develops into a whole range of miaows, which owners soon learn to recognize, from insistent mewing meaning 'I want my tea' to a more gentle greeting when you arrive home. Taking your cat to the vet may be one time when your cat will talk non-stop, indicating his displeasure and fear. Some breeds of cat are very talkative, while others may 'talk' only rarely.

Growling and hissing

While hissing demonstrates fear and distress, growling is a sign of deep anger and is a warning that a cat is about to attack.

Be wary of a hissing or growling cat.

Sleeping and dreaming

Cats are superb at sleeping. They can curl up for a nap almost anywhere and seem to fall asleep instantly, hence our use of the term 'catnap' to describe a brief sleep. The amount a cat sleeps varies according to the weather, hunger and age of the cat, and the need to mate, but on average they manage 16 hours a day. While asleep, cats experience a period of deep sleep similar to human sleep, when there is rapid eye movement and twitching of the muscles. The cat may make noises or chatter his teeth as well. This period of deep sleep can last for up to 8 minutes before the cat moves into a lighter sleep phase.

Cats will clean themselves thoroughly every day and have an established order, starting with one part of their body and methodically cleaning each area.

Seeking privacy

Cats are essentially solitary animals, living and hunting alone in the wild, and your pet cat will also need privacy. Make sure there are places he can go where he knows he won't be disturbed.

Grooming

Cats are fastidious creatures and thoroughly clean themselves every day, but it is not simply for personal

⚠ Never wake a cat suddenly, or put your face near to a sleeping cat. Disorientated, the cat will defend himself, lashing out before he realizes you are not a danger to him.

hygiene: grooming has other functions too. Applying moisture in the form of saliva to the coat helps to cool down the body, which is why you will see your cat grooming more in warm weather. Licking also stimulates glands in the skin that waterproof the fur, and cats also ingest a small amount of vitamin D while grooming.

Grooming tends to follow a set pattern, with the cat moving around his body in a methodical manner. A cat's tongue is covered in rough barbs, which serve as a brush to help groom the coat thoroughly. The very short front teeth are used to nibble at the fur to loosen and remove debris, while the forelegs are licked and then used to clean the head and ears.

Paradoxically, grooming can indicate either complete relaxation or intense anxiety. A relaxed cat will groom to clean his fur, taking time to complete each section.

He may purr as he grooms, indicating how relaxed he feels. Yet an anxious or puzzled cat will also groom. This can be compared to a nervous person fiddling with their hair or biting their nails, and is called 'displacement activity'. The biological explanation may be that fear has increased the cat's heart rate, so raising the body temperature, and grooming is used as a means of cooling the body.

Kneading

Some owners find the rhythmic kneading of their cat's front paws in their lap extremely annoying. However, this behaviour is a clear signal from the cat that he is totally relaxed and happy. The kneading mimics the behaviour of a kitten at his mother's nipple when he presses with his paws to assist the flow of milk to the teat.

Showing frustration

You may see your cat exhibit strange behaviour as he watches birds through the window, going through the motions of hunting, tensing his muscles and lashing his tail while his teeth chatter in excitement. This indicates that his hunting instincts are repressed and he feels frustration at not being able to catch the prey.

'Flehming'

When a cat catches a particularly strong or interesting smell, he wants more information than can be gained through his nose. To absorb more detail, he will inhale the air, opening his mouth in a sneering gesture as he does so. This is known as the Flehmen response, or flehming. The molecules containing the smell are drawn across the taste buds on the tongue, which is then pressed back on to the Jacobson's organ, which relays the chemical information to the hypothalamus in the brain. Flehming is particularly evident in toms that are trailing queens on heat.

Playing

Play develops the skills of hunting through stalking, pouncing, swatting, jumping and death grips. Kitten siblings will continue to develop these skills up to the age of about 5 months, when the frequency and duration of play sessions decrease. This play also teaches kittens how to interact with other cats, and develops fighting techniques for more aggressive fights as adults. Similarly, most cats enjoy play sessions with their owners where the toys take the place of prey.

Playing is an essential part of a kitten's development. It is when he learns the skills necessary for hunting and fighting later in life.

Enjoying catnip

Some plants contain chemicals that cats find irresistible and the best known of these is catnip (*Nepeta*). The leaves of catnip contain a chemical called nepetalctone. Cats will sniff, chew and roll on the plant, sending themselves into a state of intense pleasure during which they will exhibit signs of a female cat on heat – rolling, flehming and kneading. The reaction lasts about 15 minutes and, although the effect seems quite dramatic, it is quite harmless.

Around 50 per cent of cats respond to catnip, while the other half are not affected by it. If you plant catnip in your garden, it will be chewed and trampled, so be prepared to replace mutilated plants.

Catnip is used in many cat soft toys, and is also available in a spray to encourage cats to use their scratch post.

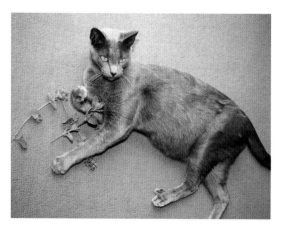

Covering their waste

Mothers are excellent teachers and show their kittens how to use the litter tray at an early age. A cat first digs a small hollow in which to deposit the waste, and then covers the waste by scraping litter over the top. He will intermittently stop and sniff the area to check that the smell of waste is covered.

Despite popular opinion, this behaviour is not because cats are extremely clean creatures. It is actually a sign of submission. In feral groups, the dominant tom will leave his faeces (and scent) on display, while those lower down the social order carefully cover theirs. By burying their waste, pet cats are acknowledging that their owners are their social superiors.

Appearing to have a sixth sense

Many people believe that cats have a sixth sense. In research it has been shown that some cats will become alert and watchful shortly before the return of their owner, even though the times may vary. Cats have also been known to exhibit signs of stress and a desire to flee before an earthquake strikes. This may be because they are highly sensitive to vibrations in the ground.

Left: Catnip has an amazing effect on a cat. After sniffing or chewing the leaves he will go into a state of intense pleasure.

Right: A cat's territory will include high vantage points from which he can view potential intruders.

Territorial behaviour

It is very important for a cat to establish and mark his territory, thereby communicating with other cats in the area, and this gives rise to several types of behaviour that owners will need to understand. Some forms of territorial behaviour can be misconstrued as deliberate naughtiness, when in fact your cat is simply trying to indicate to you that he is unhappy.

Scent messaging

Scent is vital to communication between cats, which is why they have scent organs located around their body – on the chin, cheeks, temples and at the base of the tail. Cats recognize each other by scent, and cats who know each other will greet by sniffing the head and anal regions. Cats who are very friendly will rub each other to scent mark them for future recognition.

Another form of scent messaging is 'spraying', when the cat ejects a forceful spray of urine on to an object. An unneutered tom has very strong-smelling urine, which is a powerful message to other toms in the area. Neutered males and females also spray, but the urine does not have such a strong smell.

Cats will often 'spray' objects and areas to mark out their territory. This forceful spray of strong-smelling urine provides a clear warning to other cats that they have wandered on to another cat's patch.

Territories

A cat's territory or home range is determined by a number of factors including the presence of other cats and food availability. In rural areas a cat's home range may be more than 40 hectares (100 acres), but in urban areas it is unlikely to be bigger than his own garden and the ones on either side. Females and neutered males will have a much smaller home range than an unneutered male. The range will include favourite spots for sleeping, sunbathing and keeping watch. Hunting ranges extend much further still, and may overlap other cats' hunting ranges. These ranges are flexible and are determined by the arrival of new, younger or unneutered cats.

A cat will 'mark' you by rubbing his chin and flank against you. It's a sign of friendship and an indication that you are an accepted part of his territory.

The boundaries of the home range are marked by scent and visual signals in the form of scratch marks. These messages tell visiting cats that the area is occupied, who the cat was (from previous experience) and how recently the cat scent messages have been renewed. If the scent is old, the visiting cat may feel safe to proceed; if it has been left recently, he may decide it is safer to avoid a confrontation and move in a different direction. Cats are unlikely to attack each other physically when they come face to face. After an exchange of hissing and staring, the weaker cat will usually back down by breaking eye contact first.

Problems occur when new cats are brought into the area. The owner's garden may already have been claimed by other cats, and the new cat may have to fight to gain his territory. This can lead to behavioural problems for the new cat (see page 171).

Marking in the home

You will see your cat rubbing against objects in the home, particularly when a new piece of furniture arrives, or even against bags of shopping. He first familiarizes himself with the smell of the object before marking it as part of his territory. These scent marks will be renewed frequently, particularly after a cat has been outside or if the object has been cleaned by the owner.

You may think that your cat is demonstrating his affection for you as he rubs his chin against you. In a way it is a form of friendship, because what he is doing is leaving his scent on you and marking you as a friend. Similar greetings and marking can be seen between cats in the same household, and indeed between a cat and a dog. However, this is a sign of trust and will happen only when a cat has bonded fully with the other animals.

Behaviour problems

In the wild, cats can simply move away from situations they are not happy with, but pet cats have little choice: they must suffer the problem, though they will express their dissatisfaction through a change in their behaviour. Some cats will follow their natural instincts, however, and simply leave home. By recognizing problems quickly, you will be able to avoid such extreme measures.

New arrivals

A cat often exhibits signs of anxiety when he arrives at his new home. Hiding under furniture and refusing to interact, biting and scratching are all signs that a cat is unhappy, as are refusing to eat or inappropriate toilet behaviour (using places other than the litter tray). However, given time to settle in, he should stop this behaviour. How long depends on the cat, how old he is and his previous life. A kitten should settle in quickly, whereas a semi-feral cat, which is unused to living in a house, may take a year or more to adapt.

Introductions to resident cats

Although the new cat may settle in well, a resident cat may not be so happy to have another feline in the house. Make sure the cats are correctly introduced (see pages 139–140). It is vital that the routine of the resident cat remains the same and that you show him extra love and affection during the settling-in period. Don't move his bed, litter tray or food bowls to accommodate the new arrival, and try to ensure he is not ejected from his favourite sleeping areas.

Cats feel safe when they are high up, so try to provide places, such as on top of wardrobes, for your new cat to retreat to.

Top tip

Never shout or hit your cat when he is 'naughty': he won't understand why you are reacting in that way. Instead, take the time to find the cause and continue to show your cat affection to make him feel safe in his home.

It takes time for cats to bond and initially there may be confrontations while they establish a pecking order.

Inappropriate toilet behaviour

This is one of the most common behavioural problems experienced by cat owners and its causes are numerous (see below), but it is a sure sign that the cat is unhappy with some aspect of his home. A cat who normally uses a litter tray will start to urinate and defecate in other places, usually in a corner or under a bed.

Be warned that inappropriate toilet behaviour may be a sign that your cat is ill, so you should take him to the vet immediately for a thorough medical check-up.

Inappropriate toilet activity can also be a sign of annoyance. In one case, two cats used to complete freedom via the cat flap were trapped inside the house when the cat flap became stuck shut. When the owner returned to the house, she found a pile of faeces in the middle of the sofa – a clear sign that the cats were exceedingly annoyed at being unable to go outside.

Common causes and what to do

- The litter is uncomfortable for the cat to walk on. If you have recently changed to a different type of litter, try going back to the old one.
- The cat feels vulnerable in his litter tray. This could be because the litter tray is in an area with a high level of traffic. Try siting it in a place where he will feel more private and can relieve himself in peace.
- The cat has to share his litter tray with a new cat. Always provide a litter tray for each cat.

- The cat cannot gain access to his litter tray. Make sure his litter tray is somewhere he can always get to.
- The litter tray is dirty. Always clean out waste litter daily, but don't remove it all for the first few days as the smell of his urine will attract the cat to his tray.
- The cat is marking his territory (see below).

Marking

Marking takes two forms: spraying and middening.

- Spraying is a form of territorial marking. Cats spray (eject a squirt of urine) at an object such as a fence post, bush or tree as a means of outlining the boundaries of his territory (see pages 164–165). Spraying inside the home is a sign of insecurity: the cat feels the need constantly to reinforce the boundaries of his home.
- Middening occurs when there are no problems with the litter tray, but the cat deliberately defecates or urinates in a place other than his litter tray, usually in a prominent position such as the middle of a room or on the owner's bed.

Both types of behaviour may be caused by any kind of perceived threat by the cat, such as an intruding cat, a new baby, adult or pet in the house, or even new furniture or redecoration.

What to do

- First clean the area thoroughly using biological washing powder. Many cleaners contain ammonia

Case study

Tiddy was introduced into a house with a resident cat. Introductions had gone well and Tiddy had a cat pen she could retreat to for privacy. Initially she used her litter tray without any problems. However, after a few weeks (and now allowed access to the house) she refused to use her litter tray and relieved herself on furniture and carpets.

The problem was resolved when the owner bought a covered litter tray. Tiddy was expressing her anxiety at relieving herself in the open where she might be attacked by the other cat. By providing a covered litter tray, her owner was giving Tiddy the privacy and safety she needed.

or chlorine, which the cat will associate with urine, prompting him to mark the area again.
- To keep out an intruding cat, lock the cat flap, or change it to one with a magnetic door that can be opened only by a tag on the resident cat's collar.
- Confine the cat to one room, or even a cat pen, to make him feel more secure and to break the cycle.
- Try reintroducing the cat to the new adult or pet.
- Remain calm, patient and loving.
- Never 'rub' his nose in the mess. This will only cause more stress and a continuation of the problem.

Feeding problems

Refusal to eat can have a number of causes, including illness. If your cat has not eaten for more than 24 hours, take him to the vet. If he has refused food for a shorter period, check the following possible causes.

Behaviour

Common causes and what to do

- Dislike of food. Cats can be very fussy eaters and will starve themselves rather than eat the food you provide. However, don't give in. Try placing the bowl on the floor for a few minutes, then, if the cat refuses to eat, pick it up. Put fresh food down at the next mealtime.
- The food bowl is too close to another animal's feeding point. Nervous cats may feel too intimidated to eat, so move the bowl to another area.
- The feeding area is too noisy. Make sure your cat can eat in peace.
- His food bowl is too near his litter tray. Being fastidious creatures, cats like to keep their eating area well away from their toilet area.
- If your cat is not losing weight or is even gaining weight, a neighbour may also be feeding your cat. Check to see who is feeding him and politely point out that he will become obese if they don't stop.
- Hot and humid weather can affect the appetite of your cat, but he will begin to eat more when the weather cools.

Pica

This is the term used to describe the sucking and chewing of inappropriate objects. It is seen most often in Siamese and Asian cats, but any cat can develop the habit. Often a favourite blanket will be the prime target, but it can extend to any material and some cats will destroy clothes, furniture and fabric in the home. Boredom, particularly affecting indoor cats, is often the cause. Regular play sessions to entertain and exercise the cat may help. Stimulate your cat's natural instincts by hiding food around the home so that the cat has to 'hunt' his meal.

Natural fibres such as cotton and wool should pass through the body, but manmade fibres, or large amounts of cloth, can become impacted in the stomach and intestines and will need to be removed surgically.

A cat may refuse to eat initially, but should soon demand food when he is hungry.

Your cat's pupils will widen and his ears flatten as he prepares to attack. Learn to watch out for signs that he is getting over-stimulated and stop playing until he calms down.

Aggression

Owners often find it amusing when a kitten 'attacks' their hand, but unless this behaviour is stopped it can develop into habitual aggression as the cat grows older. The cat feels rewarded for his aggressive attacks, even if it is merely the attention he receives in the response you give him as you cry out in pain.

⚠ Cats have razor-sharp teeth and claws as well as lightning reflexes, so can inflict serious wounds. Never leave a baby or toddler in a room with a cat, however well you know him. A cat will, justifiably, defend himself against a tormentor who is pulling his tail.

What to do

- Prevent aggression from developing by putting your kitten on the floor when he bites you.
- If your cat lashes out, ignore him completely. Leave the room and return in a short while, when you should immediately distract him with a toy. Never use food, or your cat may see it as a reward.

Other cats

The invasion of alien cats into a feline's home or garden can cause a number of behavioural problems. Some cats will begin to avoid areas of the home or may move upstairs and refuse to come down, demonstrating the instinctive flight instinct to avoid confrontation. Other cats may display their anxiety with inappropriate toilet behaviour, or by spraying as a means of reinforcing

Case study

When Lizzie's owners moved house, the 11-year-old cat settled in well but after a couple of months started demanding more attention in the form of play. However, when the owners responded her mood changed and she growled at them. Lizzie's home was being invaded by a neighbouring cat and Lizzie felt as though her territory was being compromised. She sought reassurance that her owners and the house were still part of her territory. Seeking play and then displaying aggression showed the conflict Lizzie was experiencing.

The house was secured against the intruding cat, and Lizzie began to feel more secure in her home. Regular play sessions and extra attention gave Lizzie the reassurance she needed, but her owners played with her on their own terms, not when she demanded it, and would cease playing if she became aggressive.

their territory. In this case, it is essential that you exclude the alien cat from your home or garden.

Garden

Try keeping a careful watch for the intruding cat, and, when he approaches, squirt him with a jet of water from a water pistol or blow a whistle loudly. He will quickly retreat. This rejection must be consistent. Don't let him see you, or he will soon learn that when you aren't there the path is clear.

If you know who the owner is, you may be able to come to an agreement about allotted times when each cat will be let out. Then your cat won't come into contact with the intruding cat and may learn to feel safer.

If this is not an option, and you cannot deter the intruder, you may have to enclose your garden by building an overhang on the top of the fences or walls. This means your cat cannot get out which will curtail his freedom. But it also means that although other cats may be able to get into the garden, they won't be able to get out and are unlikely to try to repeat the experience.

Home

Some cats will enter homes via open windows or cat flaps. This is an invasion of your cat's territory and is unacceptable. Keep windows closed and ensure you install a cat flap with a magnetic door, so that only your cat can open it. If the intruder is a feral or stray cat, contact your nearest cat-rescue centre, who will advise you on the best course of action.

Crying

Some cats just won't take 'no' for an answer; whether it is for food, a warm lap or attention, they cry until they get what they want. When owners respond to the cries of their cat, often with food or treats, they simply reinforce the behaviour. When you first get your cat, you may be unsure about his needs, but try to ignore his cries; if he has been fed, has a clean litter tray or the cat flap is open, then he may just want attention.

Behaviour

Behaviour

Attention seeking

Many owners allow their cats to have free rein of the house during the night but are then consistently woken at dawn by the cat wanting to play, to be fed or to be let out. To break this pattern, when you go to bed, shut the cat in a suitable room with access to his bed, food, water, toys and his litter tray. Put down a snack to distract him while you leave the room and shut the door. Ignore the cries, regardless of how desperate they sound. It may take two or three nights, or even a week, before your cat learns that you won't respond. You must harden your heart and put up with a few nights of broken sleep – you will be glad that you have when your cat settles down.

Over-grooming

A cat that repeatedly licks and grooms his body until the area is bare and raw is over-grooming. Other signs are sucking at the paws, tail and nipples. First take your cat to the vet to check he does not have an allergy that is making him itch. If he is physically healthy, then the most likely cause is severe boredom. To stimulate your cat, try to increase the amount of time you spend playing with him. If you have only one cat, you may want to consider getting a companion cat. A cat may also over-groom if he is stressed. Try to find the cause and correct it. Over-grooming can be habit-forming, so it is important to break the cycle early on.

Behaviour

Above and right: Sofas (and carpets) are perfect for stropping claws, and it can be difficult to persuade a cat to use his scratch post instead.

Scratching furniture

Even cats with access to trees and fence posts will use the edges of armchairs and sofas to strop their claws, simply because they are ideal for the purpose. Provide your cat with a scratch post and rub catnip on it to encourage him to use it. When you see him scratching the sofa, take him to his scratch post and 'strop' his paws for him. He may look at you in bewilderment initially, but if you are consistent he should soon get the message. Give him plenty of toys to play with and cardboard boxes to scratch and chew. If this does not work, you will have to confine him to less smart areas of the house where it does not matter if the furniture or carpet get scratched.

Don't replace a worn-out scratch post until absolutely necessary. The loose fibres are ideal for the cat to scratch and his smell is impregnated on the post. If you make a scratch post yourself, don't use leftover carpet from the sitting room as it will confuse the cat; he may see it as permission to use the carpet rather than his scratch post.

HEALTH

Generally, cats are independent animals. Quick and agile, they rarely have an accident, and with a healthy diet and proper care they can live for many years without illness. However, it is important that you can recognize when your cat is unwell, which means getting to know his body and normal behaviour. Many symptoms of ill health are manifested in a change in behaviour.

Signs of ill health

- Reluctance to eat
- Lethargy
- Visible haw (third eyelid)
- Runny nose or eyes
- Coughing and sneezing
- Diarrhoea or vomiting
- Constipation
- Frequent urination
- Pain when touched
- Stiffness or difficulty in movement
- Failure to groom
- Scratching or licking
- Swollen abdomen
- Weight loss or gain
- Marked change in behaviour such as unexpected aggression
- Increase or decrease in thirst
- Blood in faeces or urine
- Shaking of head/pawing at ears

Choosing a vet

It is important to be confident in your vet's abilities. So, if possible, choose a vet who specializes in feline medicine. The clinic should be as close to your home as possible; generally, cats don't like travelling, so the shorter the journey, especially in an emergency, the better. Ask friends and family if they know of a good vet, or check with your local rescue centre to find out who they would recommend.

If you are concerned about your vet's diagnosis, don't be afraid to seek a second opinion, which your vet can arrange for you. He may even recommend that you see a specialist for your cat's medical condition.

After a visit to your vet, your cat will smell very different to other animals in the household and will be quite stressed by his experience. This can cause unwelcome curiosity or even hostility and can lead to fights between cats that are normally friends. Reintroduce the cat to the other animals by separating him and exchanging scents as you would with a new cat. This will help to disguise the scent from the veterinary surgery. It will also give the cat time to relax and recover from his visit to the vet.

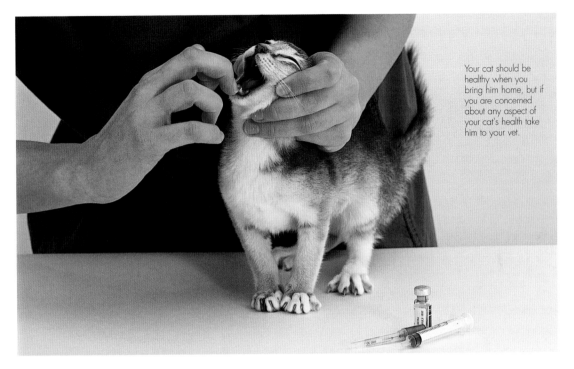

Your cat should be healthy when you bring him home, but if you are concerned about any aspect of your cat's health take him to your vet.

Regular checks

Try to set aside time once a week for an all-over health check. It is much easier if you start doing this when your pet is still a kitten, so he can get used to you examining him thoroughly.

Check the fur for fleas, ticks or other parasites. Use a flea comb to check for flea eggs. Gently feel the cat's body for signs of lumps, scabs or cuts. The coat should be clean and glossy. Check that the eyes are clear and bright, and free from discharge. The inside of the ears should be free from excessive wax. Gently open the mouth and examine the teeth. The breath should not smell; the gums should be a salmon-pink colour.

How to keep your cat healthy

To give him the best possible chance of a happy, healthy existence, follow these rules:

- Feed him the correct food.
- Ensure he has plenty of exercise.
- Worm and deflea him on a regular basis.
- Take him for his vaccinations.
- Give him a weekly home check-up.
- Take him to the vet as soon as you think he may be ill.
- Keep his bed and food bowls clean.
- Clear waste from his litter tray every day.
- Give him plenty of love.

Food and drink

Feeding your cat a healthy, well-balanced diet will help him to live a long and happy life. Pet-food manufacturers invest large sums of money in producing food that contains the correct number of vitamins and minerals for specific age groups and pedigree types. Once you have selected the correct food for your cat, read the packaging carefully and follow the guidelines.

Feeding your cat

Refer to the feeding chart opposite to find out how much and how often you should feed your kitten or cat during the different stages of his life. Your kitten should be at least 12 weeks old when you collect him, and already eating food formulated for kittens, but he will still require several small meals a day.

In the wild, adult cats eat 'mouse-sized' portions of food and so have several small meals a day. Some cats like to snack frequently and return to their bowl several times to finish their food, while other cats will eat the entire meal in one go. It is a good idea to feed twice a day, once in the morning and again in the evening, as spacing the meals establishes a routine and provides regular meals of fresh food. Incidentally, in the wild cats eat freshly killed prey, which is still slightly warm, so cats tend to prefer food that is at room temperature and will often refuse to eat food taken directly from a fridge.

Cats over the age of 8 years are classed as entering old age. As cats age, their metabolism becomes less efficient and it may be necessary to feed two or more meals a day, depending on your cat's condition.

Feeding bowls

Ceramic, stainless steel and plastic bowls are available. Check that the bowl cannot slide around the floor while the cat is eating. Some cats are messy eaters, lifting food from the bowl and placing it on the floor to chew. Try putting a mat under the bowl to protect the floor.

Types of food

The following types of food are available:

- Wet food – available in cans or pouches
- Semi-moist food – available in pouches
- Dry food – available in bags

Wet and semi-moist foods contain a high percentage of water, satisfying to a large degree the fluid requirements of a cat. Dry food has the advantage of remaining fresh all day but your cat will need extra water.

Try to provide a varied diet. Pedigree cats often have very delicate stomachs, however, so use foods that are formulated specifically for their needs.

Don't feed dog food to your cat: it does not contain the correct balance of nutrients and proteins a cat needs.

Cats cannot be vegetarians. They need an essential amino acid called taurine, which the cat's body cannot produce and which is provided by a meat diet. A deficiency in taurine can lead to visual impairment, infertility and heart disease.

Treats

These are very high in calories, so be careful not to give too many or you may soon have an overweight cat on your hands. Always read the packet carefully, and give only the number of treats advised by the manufacturer. Alternatively, save some dry food from your cat's meal to use as treats during the day.

It's all too easy to reward a cat with food, but even a small number of treats each day could lead to obesity.

LIFE-STAGE FEEDING

Age	Feeding regime
Under 8 weeks	Kittens start being weaned off their mother's milk at 4–5 weeks; by the age of 8 weeks they should be eating solid food
8–12 weeks (3 months)	5 small (25 g/1 oz) meals a day of kitten food
3–5 months	4 small meals a day of kitten food
5–6 months	3 meals a day
6–12 months	2 meals a day
12 months–8 years	1–2 meals a day
Over 8 years	1–2 meals a day, but increase to 2 or more if advised by your vet

Drink

You should provide clean drinking water every day. However, cats will often ignore the fresh water on offer and wander outside to lap up dirty water from a puddle. The reason for this is that tap water contains chemicals, which the cat can taste. Left for a few hours, the taste of the chemicals diminishes and the cat is more likely to use the bowl of water. Puddles, though dirty, are not contaminated with chemicals and more to a cat's taste.

Milk

Many cats enjoy drinking milk and suffer no ill effects, but some cats cannot tolerate the lactose in cow's milk and suffer diarrhoea as a consequence of drinking it. Instead, give your cat special 'cat's milk', which is lactose-reduced but still contains calcium.

Drinking bowls

Cats are fussy creatures, and where one bowl will suit one cat another will refuse to drink from it. Many cats like to drink from dripping taps, or from a glass filled with water. Cats often prefer wide, flat bowls that can accommodate their whiskers. There are also products such as cat water fountains that automatically fill the bowl when it is almost empty, ensuring fresh water is always available to your cat.

Never use washing-up liquid when washing the drinking bowl. Even though the bowl has been rinsed, cats, who have a highly developed sense of taste, will taste detergent in the water.

Obesity

The number of obese cats is increasing rapidly. Obesity is often caused by well-intentioned owners responding to the pleas of their cat for more food. Part of the problem is due to developments in the production of cat food, which is made to be as tasty as possible. It would appear that cats are losing the ability to control their intake, craving more of the food they enjoy.

Obesity is also more prevalent in cats kept as indoor pets. Constrained by their environment, indoor cats tend not to exercise enough, failing to burn up the calories they are taking in. Indoor cats may also eat more as a result of boredom.

To avoid your cat getting overweight, follow these rules:

- Feed only the amount of food recommended on the packet or can.
- Save some of his food to use as treats.
- Don't give your cat fattening food such as cream or cheese, except as a very occasional treat.
- Set aside time each day to play with your cat.
- Try dividing his meal into several smaller portions so that he does not get hungry between meals.
- If you have two cats, feed them separately to ensure that the obese cat does not have access to the other cat's food as well as his own.
- If you are concerned about your cat's weight, consult your vet. Many surgeries now run specific clinics for overweight pets, which offer advice and support.

Some cats prefer to drink water from a dripping tap. Others like a glass of water, while many cats simply drink from puddles outside.

Health

Vaccinations and pills

Cats are susceptible to viral diseases, some of which can be fatal. With an increase in the number of cats living in relatively small areas, these diseases are becoming more prevalent, so it is more important than ever that your cat is vaccinated. It is also important that, when necessary, you will be able to administer pills to your cat.

Protecting against disease

Disease can be transferred via other cats through the air, through mating or other physical contact, or in the womb by a mother to her kittens. Your cat should be vaccinated against the following diseases:

- Feline leukaemia virus (FeLV)
- Cat 'flu (feline respiratory disease). There are two viral forms of this disease comprising feline herpes virus (FHV) – also known as feline viral rhinotracheitus (FVR) – and feline calici virus (FCV)
- Feline infectious enteritis (also known as feline panleukopenia)
- Feline chlamydia

Other vaccinations will be required if you are planning to take your cat abroad, including a vaccination for rabies. Vaccination for feline infectious peritonitis (FIP) is currently available only in the USA. Vaccinations are now generally given in a combined injection.

Indoor cats should also be vaccinated in case they escape or in case a new cat, which may carry a virus, is introduced into the house.

When to vaccinate

Kittens are first vaccinated when they are about 9 weeks old, with the second dose given at 12 weeks. Full protection is achieved around 7–10 days after the second vaccination. Annual boosters will continue to offer protection against disease. If you are planning to board your cat, or to travel abroad, you will need to provide proof that he has been vaccinated.

Risks

There are risks associated with vaccinations, but adverse reactions are rare. There may be a small lump at the injection site and the cat may be lethargic and refuse to eat for a day after immunization. If you are concerned, contact your vet for advice. Many insurance companies will not pay for treatment if a cat is not vaccinated, so check your policy details carefully.

Administering pills

It can be difficult to administer pills, such as worming tablets, to a reluctant cat. Try the following methods (it is useful to have an assistant if your cat is uncooperative). If you are unsure or it proves impossible, ask your veterinary nurse to show you the best method.

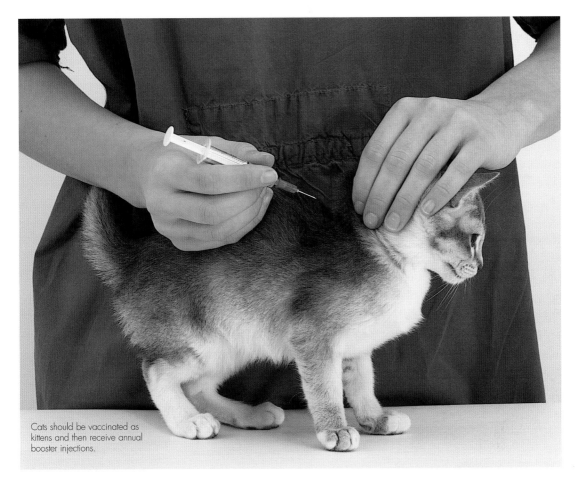

Cats should be vaccinated as kittens and then receive annual booster injections.

- Restrain the cat by wrapping him in a towel so that his legs are held firmly and only his head is free.
- Place the finger and thumb of one hand on each side of his jaw and press gently. This will make him open his mouth.
- With your other hand drop the pill to the back of his throat.
- Hold his mouth closed and gently rub his throat to encourage him to swallow.

Alternatively, you can disguise tablets by crushing them and mixing them with his food. Some tablets have a strong taste, so you may need to mix the pill with strong-smelling food, such as tuna, to disguise the taste. Chilling the pill in the fridge beforehand can reduce the flavour.

Always check with your vet before crushing a pill, however. The efficacy of some medications is reduced when they are crushed.

Parasite control

Cats, particularly those with access to the outdoors, are vulnerable to infestation by external and internal parasites, and you will need to take preventative measures to protect your cat. If you regularly treat him for parasites, they need not be a problem. Ask your vet for suitable treatments for fleas, worms, ticks and mites.

Fleas

These insects bite the host's skin and feed on blood, after which they jump off to find another host to prey on. Fleas breed prolifically. The adult lives on the host, laying eggs at a rate of up to 50 a day. The eggs fall on to the floor where the larva move away from the light into carpets and upholstery. In the right conditions, adult fleas hatch after two to three weeks. A severe infestation of fleas on a kitten can lead to anaemia. Ask your vet about suitable flea-control treatments for kittens.

Two lines of action are necessary: treating both the cat and the house. There are a number of different flea treatments available for treating cats.

- Flea collars – these are impregnated with chemicals that kill fleas, but collars can irritate the skin, leading to loss of hair around the neck.
- Powder – this is easy to administer, but is generally not a long-lasting treatment.
- Spray – choose the pump-action bottles, rather than aerosol cans, which can 'hiss' and frighten the cat. It may be difficult to make the cat stand still for long enough to cover the body thoroughly.
- Drop-on – the easiest method, drop-on (or spot-on) flea treatments are administered from a pipette to the back of the neck.

Left: Continual scratching is a sign of fleas.

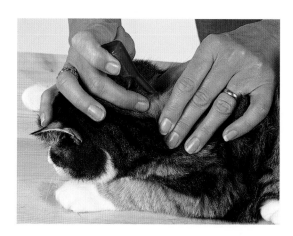

Right: Drop-on flea treatments are the easiest to administer.

You will also need to treat the house. Sprays are available from your vet that will prevent flea infestation for 6–12 months. Wash your pet's bedding and vacuum carpets regularly to destroy flea eggs.

Worms

Cats that hunt and eat prey are most at risk of catching worms. Tapeworm and roundworm are the most common types in the UK. Heartworms and hookworms are prevalent in large parts of Europe, though not in the UK, so cats living in these areas will require treatment against these worms. In the USA and other parts of the world, hookworms, whipworms, threadworms and heartworms may infect cats. The most effective treatments are available from your vet, who will advise you on how frequently your cat needs to be treated. A hunting cat will need to be treated every 2–3 months.

Ticks

These are relatively uncommon in cats because they self-groom so efficiently, but cats living in rural areas may pick up ticks on their fur while walking through long grass. The tick, which looks like a small bluish-grey bean, is an eight-legged parasite that grips the skin with mouth hooks. As it sucks the blood from the cat, its body swells from almost flat to rounded when it is fully engorged. Never try to pull off a tick as you may leave the mouth hooks behind; this can cause an infection.

There are specific treatments available, and some flea treatments are suitable for use on ticks too. Alternatively, you can use a tick remover, which hooks under the tick's

⚠ Never use more than one type of treatment at the same time, as you may overdose your cat. Never use treatments intended for other animals on your cat – cats can die if given flea treatment intended for dogs.

body and enables it to be removed quickly before the tick has a chance to hold tight.

Mites

There are several different types of mite, all of which are minute and can be detected only by the symptoms, which include dandruff, itching and bald patches. Your vet will be able to identify the type of mite on your cat and prescribe some medication to cure him.

Ticks may be picked up by cats that have access to areas of long grass.

Other considerations

In addition to vaccinations and parasite control, there are many other aspects of your cat's health of which you will need to be aware, including ringworm, furballs and dental care. Unless you are planning to breed from a pedigree cat, it is vital that you neuter your cat to prevent unwanted kittens. Neutering can also prevent straying, fighting and spraying.

Ringworm

Despite its name, this is caused by a fungus, not a worm. It is spread by direct contact, or via an object that has been in contact with a contaminated animal. Symptoms are small, round, hairless patches on the face, head, ears, forepaws and back, which cause mild irritation. Otherwise the cat is not usually affected. Ringworm can affect humans, so it is important to seek veterinary advice as soon as symptoms are seen, which will be 2–4 weeks after infection.

Furballs (hairballs)

A furball or hairball is an accumulation of hair in the cat's stomach. Ingested hair usually passes harmlessly through the body, but if there is excessive hair loss, particularly during moulting, hair can accumulate and form a solid mass, which rubs against the lining of the stomach. The resulting irritation will cause the cat to vomit up the mass. If you see your cat crouching on the floor and coughing (or retching) repeatedly with his neck extended, he is probably trying to cough up a furball. Eventually he should vomit a soggy ball of matted hair.

Ringworm is highly infectious and can be passed on to humans.

Health

Cleaning your cat's teeth can help to prevent the build-up of tartar.

Sometimes, the mass lodges further down the digestive tract and will cause a blockage, leading to constipation, a loss of appetite and lethargy. If your cat exhibits these symptoms, take him to the vet. Grooming regularly will help to avoid furballs.

Teeth

A kitten has 28 milk teeth, which he will lose at around the age of 4 months. An adult cat has 30 teeth, 16 in the upper jaw and 14 in the lower jaw. It is not known why some cats suffer from dental problems while others remain problem-free, though scientists now believe it may be due to genetics.

Teeth should be clean and white and the gums a pale pink colour. Cats can suffer from a build-up of tartar on their teeth, which, if untreated, can lead to gingivitis (inflammation of the gums) and to infection and loss of teeth. Early detection is essential to minimize the damage and prevent tooth loss, so ensure your cat has an annual dental examination.

Products for cleaning pets' teeth are now available in the form of meat-flavoured toothpaste and small soft brushes. It is advisable to start brushing your cat's teeth from a young age when he is easier to handle. Dental chews are also available, which are designed to remove debris from the teeth, helping to clean them.

Neutering

Unless you plan to breed from your pedigree cat, or have homes planned for any kittens, you should neuter your cat at around 6 months old for male kittens and 4–5 months old for female kittens. Breeding requires commitment and care on the part of the owner. If you want to breed from your cat, or you think she may be pregnant, seek advice from your vet, who will be able to explain fully the necessary care for the mother and kittens. Many people believe it is better for a female cat to have a litter before she is neutered, but there is no medical evidence that giving birth to a litter of kittens is beneficial to a cat.

Here are five good reasons to neuter your cat:

- **Unwanted cats and kittens** – there are far too many of these looking for loving homes.
- **Straying** – unneutered cats are driven to find mates. A tom, in particular, will be desperate to find females with which he can mate and thereby pass on his genes.
- **Injuries** – unneutered toms are more aggressive and will fight to defend their territory from other toms.

- **Disease** – unneutered cats may mate with unvaccinated feral cats and so be at risk of picking up a disease.
- **Spraying** – unneutered toms spray more, and their urine is very pungent.

Toxoplasmosis

This disease can cause great concern to cat owners, particularly those with young children, or pregnant women. Cats can be infected with the *Toxoplasma gondii* parasite when they eat prey, and the eggs of the microscopic parasite are then shed in the cat's faeces. Infection is harmless to people with a strong immune system, but the unborn and young children are most at risk. The disease can cause jaundice, enlarged liver and spleen, and convulsions. To avoid becoming infected, follow these rules:

- Always wear rubber gloves when you clean the litter tray.
- Wear gloves when digging in soil where a cat may have defecated.
- If you are pregnant, avoid doing either of the above activities.
- Cover a child's sandpit so that the cat cannot defecate there.
- Don't allow cats to walk on kitchen worktops.

If you are concerned about toxoplasmosis ask your vet for advice, but bear in mind that the people most at risk are those who handle raw meat or eat undercooked meat.

First aid

Despite a cat being an independent creature who is perfectly capable of taking care of himself, accidents can and do happen. However, if you have first-aid knowledge you will be able to help your injured cat. Some veterinary clinics run basic first-aid courses to help owners deal with accidents and emergencies.

First-aid kit

It is essential to be prepared for emergencies, so make sure you have a first-aid kit specifically for your cat, containing the following items:

- Adhesive tape – for securing bandages.
- Antiseptic fluid – for cleaning wounds.
- Bandages – for dressing wounds.
- Conforming bandage – this sticky bandage adheres to itself, making dressing wounds easier.
- Cotton buds – for cleaning wounds and for applying ointment.
- Cotton wool – for cleaning wounds.
- Curved, round-ended scissors – for clipping fur and trimming dressings.
- Elizabethan collar – to prevent the cat from scratching wounds.
- Emergency (silver foil) blanket or large sheet of 'bubble wrap' – to maintain body temperature.
- Pencil torch – to inspect ears, eyes and mouth.
- Protective gloves – to protect your hands while restraining the cat.
- Round-ended tweezers – to remove thorns or stings.
- Salt – can be used to make a saline solution for

cleaning wounds (2 tablespoons of table salt dissolved in 1 litre/1¾ pints of warm water).
- Small plastic bowl – to use for antiseptic solutions.
- Sterile dressings – choose ones with a 'clear' side that won't stick to the wound.
- Surgical gloves – to prevent infection.
- Syringe plunger – to administer liquid medicines.
- Towel – to wrap around the cat for restraining him.
- Vet's emergency telephone number.

Be prepared for an emergency by putting together a first-aid kit for your cat.

Never give human medication to a cat. A cat cannot easily detoxify and eliminate poisonous substances from his body. Aspirin can kill a cat.

Initial checks

If your cat has suffered a serious injury, such as being hit by a car, and is unconscious, you must immediately check the following: airway, breathing and circulation – which can be easily remembered as ABC.

Airway
Check that neither his tongue nor any debris is blocking his throat.

Breathing
Watch for signs of breathing, such as the rise and fall of the flank. If you are unsure if the flank is moving or not, a simple way of checking to see if the cat is still breathing is to hold a small mirror in front of his mouth and nose. If the mirror mists over, this is caused by his warm breath condensing on the mirrror.

Circulation
Check for a heartbeat by placing your ear on the left side of the cat just behind his elbow. Alternatively, put two fingers in the same place, or on the inside of the groin at the top of the rear leg.

Artificial respiration

If he is not breathing, try gently lifting his chin to extend the neck and open the airway. If this does not work, you will have to administer artificial respiration:

- Hold the cat's mouth closed with one hand and place your lips over his nose.
- Very gently breathe up the cat's nose, at a rate of 30 breaths every minute.
- Remove your mouth between each breath to allow the cat to exhale.
- Continue until a vet arrives, or until the cat begins to breathe on his own.

Chest compressions

If there is no heartbeat, you will have to administer chest compressions:

- Place one hand on either side of the cat's chest just behind his elbows.
- Squeeze the chest in a smooth action; use the flat of your hand not the fingers.
- Don't use too much force or you may break the ribs with the pressure.
- Give two compressions every second.
- Give two breaths to the cat for every four compressions.
- Keep checking the pulse and breathing.
- Keep trying until the vet arrives or until you decide the cat is beyond help.

Moving an injured cat

Wrapping a towel around the cat will help to prevent
further injuries and stop him lashing out with his claws.

An injured cat will be extremely frightened and may
struggle to get free, or lash out with his claws. Wrapping
the cat in a towel will protect you both from further
injury. Always speak calmly to the injured cat. When
you move the cat, try to keep him as still as possible to
prevent further injury. If there is a board or other rigid
object handy, slide it under the cat to keep his body flat
and stable. Alternatively, use both hands to hold him as
flat and still as possible.

Shock

This is one of the most significant factors in the death of
an animal after an accident. Signs of shock include
staring eyes, cool skin, and a faint, rapid pulse. If you
notice these signs, immediate veterinary attention is
essential. Wrap the cat in an emergency blanket or
other warm covering, and take him straight to the vet.

Other first-aid situations

Bleeding

For minor wounds, apply gentle pressure with a pad until the bleeding stops. With serious bleeding, if you can locate the artery or vein (under the skin on the heart side of the wound) apply pressure to slow the bleeding. Alternatively, press a pad on the wound to slow the bleeding and, if possible, elevate the injury.

Burns and scalds

Cool the burnt area with cold water; this will help to reduce pain and the severity of the burn. Cover the burn with a clean, damp cloth. Wrap the cat in an emergency blanket and take him to a vet immediately.

Choking

Immediate action is essential. Wrap the cat in a towel, then open his mouth to see if anything is stuck in it. If the object is wedged, don't try to remove it with your fingers, as you could simply push it further in.

- Sit on a chair, and place the cat on the floor facing away from you.
- Lift the cat's hind legs and hold them firmly between your knees.
- Place one hand on either side of the cat's chest and squeeze using a sudden, jerky movement.
- Repeat four or five times.

Immediately apply cold water to burns or scalds to cool the injury. Then cover with a clean damp cloth.

The aim is to make the cat cough out the object. If this is achieved, let the cat recover before taking him to the vet. If coughing does not remove the object, take him to the vet immediately.

Vomiting

Occasional vomiting is normal and is often the result of eating food too quickly. Intermittent vomiting may be caused by scavenging. In this case, starve your cat for 24 hours, but ensure he has access to water. If the vomiting continues during the starvation period, or once food is reintroduced, ask your vet for advice.

If your cat experiences recurrent vomiting or produces large amounts of vomit or blood in the vomit, consult your vet immediately.

Diarrhoea

Sudden runny, smelly stools may be caused by overeating or stress – starve your cat for 24 hours but ensure access to water. If the diarrhoea is persistent and frequent, take your cat to the vet. Diarrhoea can cause dehydration, which in severe cases can lead to death. Be particularly careful with kittens, who can become dehydrated quickly. If in doubt, always seek advice from your vet.

Poisoning

Symptoms are excessive salivation or frothing at the mouth, or extreme sleepiness. Call your vet immediately, and tell him what may have poisoned your cat so the surgery can obtain the relevant information about the poison. Take him to the vet immediately. You may be advised to make your cat vomit; your vet will advise you how to do this.

Drowning

Remove the cat from the water. Hold him upside down to drain the water from his lungs, gently swinging him from side to side (no more than six times). Lay him flat and rub the body vigorously to encourage him to breathe. If he is not breathing, administer artificial respiration (see page 188).

Electrocution

First turn off the power supply. Don't approach the cat until the electricity is turned off. Check if the cat is breathing; if not, administer artificial respiration (see page 188). Remember that electrocution causes burns (see opposite).

Health

Top tip

You must always ensure your own safety first. If the cat is very aggressive, or lying in a dangerous situation such as in a road, it may be advisable to wait until additional help arrives.

Hereditary problems

There are a number of diseases and conditions that may be inherited by a kitten from his parents and which are caused by a genetic fault. These diseases tend to be confined to pedigree breeds that are selectively bred. With the exception of congenital deafness, non-pedigree cats are not prone to hereditary disease. The most common feline diseases are described here.

Congenital deafness

This is caused by a dominant white gene, and it particularly affects white cats with blue eyes (but not all). There is no cure and the kitten is deaf from birth.

Eye disease

Progressive retinal atrophy damages the retina, leading to blindness. It has been found to be hereditary in Abyssinian cats.

Heart defects

Hypertrophic cardiomyopathy causes heart failure in Maine Coon cats that have inherited the disease. This condition is not present in non-pedigree cats.

Polycystic kidney disease (PKD)

Common in Persian and Exotic cats, multiple fluid-filled cysts form in the kidneys during development in the womb. The cysts grow larger but the rate at which they grow varies widely from cat to cat. Eventually they begin to interfere with the function of the kidneys and ultimately lead to renal failure. There may be no symptoms until the cysts are quite large and have already caused significant damage, and there is no treatment to prevent or cure the cysts.

A scheme to identify cats with PKD and remove them from breeding stock has been set up by the Feline Advisory Bureau in an attempt to eradicate the disease. If you are planning to acquire a Persian or Exotic kitten (or other breeds, such as British Shorthair, which may have been outcrossed with Persians), you should ask the breeder if the parents have been screened for PKD.

The Manx gene results in a tailless cat but can also cause severe abnormalities.

The kinked tail and squint of old-type Siamese cats are caused by a defective gene now largely eliminated from the breed.

Genetic problems in Manx cats

The Manx gene causes the development of the characteristically tailless cat, but it can also cause severe abnormalities in the foetus, including spina bifida. If the foetus inherits the Manx gene from both parents, it will be miscarried. Pregnancies as a result of matings between a Manx and another breed often result in a high number of stillbirths and early deaths.

Genetic problems in Siamese cats

The Siamese gene causes damage to the nerve from the eye to the brain. The damage leads to poor depth of vision and a squint as the cat attempts to see correctly. The same gene is also responsible for the kink seen in the tails of old-type Siamese. This gene has largely been bred out with the introduction of the modern Siamese type.

OLDER CAT CARE

The company of an ageing cat in good health is delightful and soothing and as rewarding as playing with a kitten. For those people who enjoy cuddling a 'lap cat', many older felines are happy to oblige, delighting in a warm lap, gentle stroking and quiet conversation. With a little extra care and affection, you can make your pet's twilight years a real pleasure for you both.

When is a cat old?

A cat can be considered old when he starts to take things easy and spends more time than usual sleeping. On average, cats now live to around 14 years of age, thanks to improved geriatric feline veterinary care and nutrition. Many cats live until their late teens, although they can look a little unkempt. But just because they sit around a lot and are undemanding and quiet, elderly cats should not be ignored.

Lifestyle

Like elderly people, old cats are resistant to and can be upset by major changes in their routine and lifestyle. If changes do have to happen, try to incorporate them gradually to allow your cat time to get used to them.

Everything should be done to keep the elderly cat feeling as good as possible. Disturbed behaviour patterns may be the result of chronic illness in the old cat. For example, a previously clean cat may have accidents, making puddles on chairs and carpets. Should this happen, it may be best to keep your pet in areas of the house where such accidents don't matter – though that does not mean he should be shut away or limited in his access to his family, as this would be unfair and cruel. It would also be unfair and cruel to chastise or ban him from the house for something that is beyond his control.

Keep an eye on senior cats when they are allowed outside, particularly senile, blind or deaf pets, since they are at risk from getting lost and from potential hazards such as predators and traffic.

Companionship

Some people consider getting a kitten when their established cat gets old. This can be a good or bad decision depending on the temperament and nature of the aged cat. If he likes the kitten, then he may gain a new lease of life. If, however, he resents the intruder, he may become depressed and withdrawn, stop eating and, ultimately, become very ill. If the old cat is the only one in the household and has always been a loner, then it would be kinder not to get another cat or kitten.

If your cat seems lonely, leaving a radio on low while you are out can help to provide your pet with 'company' through the sound of voices.

If your elderly cat displays an increased need for your company, make sure you give him plenty of attention and reassurance.

Feeding and health

It is particularly important with an older cat to feed him properly and keep a vigilant eye on his general condition. He may also need help with grooming to ensure his coat remains in good order. Watch litter tray habits: bladder and bowel problems may occur if your elderly pet is intimidated by another pet while on his tray, or if he cannot physically get on to his tray.

Diet

You can get food specially formulated for elderly cats. This contains all the nutrients the ageing body needs to remain in the best possible condition and helps to alleviate or delay the onset of conditions such as senility. As older cats can often suffer from urinary tract problems, a totally dry food diet may not be the best choice; consult your vet regarding the best type of food for your senior pet. Bad teeth and inflamed gums are not uncommon in old felines; at this stage, your cat will find soft moist or semi-moist food easier to eat. Make sure he always has a plentiful supply of fresh, clean water.

Older cats may not be as able to defend their food as they once were; so, if you have other cats and/or dogs, make sure they are not allowed to steal his meals or intimidate him while he is eating and scare him away from his food.

The fact that they are less active as they grow older means that it is easy for older cats to pile on weight. This is not good for their health, as obesity puts a strain on the heart and joints, so a careful watch must be kept for a burgeoning waistline. Equally, senior felines can lose weight rapidly and starve if they are not eating. Weighing your cat once a week can help you to monitor his weight: weigh yourself on bathroom scales and then weigh yourself while holding the cat; deduct the first weight from the second to ascertain your pet's weight. If possible, get someone to read the weights while you stand still on the scales. The ideal weight for your cat will depend on many factors, including his breed, so ask your vet for advice.

Older cats are more prone to constipation, so keep a watch for this and seek veterinary attention if it occurs.

A rotund shape and pendulous abdomen are signs that your cat is overweight.

Health

The key to good health care for your old cat lies in vigilance. Twice-yearly check-ups by your vet will alert him to early signs of problems; some vets run clinics for older cats, recognizing the need to spend a little extra time on these much-cherished companions. As a cat ages, so a certain amount of body tissue degeneration occurs. This is inevitable and cannot be prevented, although with joint owner and veterinary care the effects can be eased.

Ailments that affect senior cats

Seek veterinary advice for all of the following ailments – the quicker they are dealt with, the more likely the outcome will be successful in comfortably prolonging the cat's life.

- Coat and skin complaints due to inefficient self-grooming
- Increased predisposition to furballs
- Cold-related problems due to decreased body-temperature regulation
- Thyroid problems
- Claw wounds
- Injury due to decrease in agility
- Incontinence
- Constipation due to decreased digestive efficiency
- Obesity-related problems
- Loss of appetite
- Sight problems
- Tooth and gum problems
- Deafness
- Senility
- Joint stiffness and arthritis
- High blood pressure (hypertension)
- Heart disease
- Kidney disease
- Liver failure

Grooming

As cats age, their joints stiffen and they become less flexible. This makes it harder for them to groom hard-to-reach places, such as the back, rear of the neck and under the tail. Older cats therefore need to be groomed regularly to keep their coats in good condition.

Claws may need to be trimmed regularly if your cat is not wearing them down through exercise outside. The claws can be injured if they become caught in furnishings or clothing.

When the end comes

Eventually an older cat sleeps more and more, and is increasingly reluctant to exercise. He may drink lots of fluids but takes little food. If his bladder and bowels begin to fail and the cat is unable to eat, veterinary advice must be sought, for the only humane thing to do is to have your pet 'put down', otherwise known as euthanasia.

Don't let him suffer

Sometimes owners cannot bear to lose their pet (which is understandable) and delay having him put down, when really it should be done sooner rather than later. However, a caring owner will put their pet's needs first, not their own, whatever the emotional cost.

Other than sudden death, having a cat put down is the most humane way for him to die. While it may be upsetting to read about the process, it can help if you understand how euthanasia is achieved. Talk it over with your vet first and decide whether having it done at home or at the clinic would be the most suitable and practical option. Also discuss the options of what to do with your pet's body. Once this has been mutually agreed, then arrange a date.

At the veterinary clinic

Arrange a time when the vet clinic is likely to be quiet, or enter and leave via a private entrance so that you do not have to face a crowded waiting room. Have a supportive person drive you there and back; you may well be upset, and therefore in no fit state to undertake this yourself. Take a blanket to wrap your pet in to bring him home again, if this is what you want.

If you feel you will go to pieces, then ask your vet and the vet nurse to deal with the procedure. If you stay with your cat, your distress will upset him, and so his passing may not be as peaceful as it should be.

At home

This is the preferred option if you are unable to get to the clinic, your cat is too ill to move, he finds travel upsetting, or you would prefer euthanasia to be carried out in familiar and comfortable surroundings. Request that a veterinary nurse attends as well as the vet. The nurse can assist when required and help to keep both you and the cat calm, and therefore the process as stress-free as possible.

On the day, keep your cat's routine as normal, but give him lots of extra attention and cuddles if he is amenable to this. He will not understand why you are being extra-affectionate, but may appreciate it nonetheless, and it will make you feel better as well as making the most of those last precious moments.

Choosing a familiar spot at home for your cat's final injection may make the process easier, and more intimate. And neither you nor your cat will have to suffer the stress of going to a vet's clinic.

The process

Properly carried out, the process is quick and relatively painless. A sedative injection may be given if the cat is very distressed or is difficult to handle or restrain. A foreleg is usually shaved to identify where the relevant vein is situated. An injection is given into this vein comprising a concentrated solution of phenobarbitone (an anaesthetic overdose). In thin cats, the injection can be given directly into a kidney. The cat almost immediately goes to sleep. Breathing swiftly ceases and the heart stops beating.

In some cases the circulatory system will not be working efficiently, and therefore it will not be easy to find the necessary vein on the foreleg into which to administer the lethal injection. When this occurs, the vet may need to inject directly into the heart or kidneys. Owners can find this distressing and be unable to cope efficiently in holding their pet and keeping him calm. This is where the experienced handling and sympathetic soothing afforded by a veterinary nurse can prove beneficial to all concerned.

Afterwards

The vet will dispose of the body or arrange to have it buried or cremated on your instructions. Alternatively, you can take it home with you, if this is allowable, to bury in a favoured area of the garden. (Graves should be at least 1 m/3 ft 3 in deep and well away from watercourses – your local environment agency should be able to advise.) Pet cemeteries and crematoria will advise you on cost and what is involved.

Grief

Losing a much-loved pet is just the same for many owners as coping with the death of a family member or close friend. Individual people deal with this trauma in different ways, but all or some of the stages of grief that are often encountered, in no particular order, are: anticipation of loss, shock, denial, anger, depression and acceptance.

It is important to realize that grieving is an essential part of the healing process after bereavement. There is no set time limit as to how long owners should grieve; some are able to accept and recover from the loss more easily than others, who may not get over it for months, even years – and this is perfectly normal. However long it takes, don't be afraid to grieve when you feel the need to; bottling up grief inside you is bound to affect your own mental and physical health.

Sometimes you may feel as though you are over the loss, but then grief hits you again at unexpected moments – such as when something triggers memories of your pet – and feelings of extreme sadness engulf you all over again. This is normal. However, do not be afraid to lean on supportive family and friends when you feel the need, and do make use of the many excellent pet bereavement counselling services that are available by telephone, letter and email – many animal charities provide such a service, as do some pet insurance companies.

However hard it may be to face up to, having your old pet put down is the kindest thing you can do for a much-loved companion and friend that is suffering, to prevent him further distress.

If overwhelming sorrow persists for longer than you feel able to cope with, then consult an understanding doctor. It may be that you need additional counselling or even prescribed medication to help to ease the debilitating grief and to allow you to function with some degree of normality again.

Children and pet loss

Depending on their age, children react differently to the death of a pet. It will help enormously for a parent to talk things through with a bereavement counsellor as to how to approach and explain pet death, especially to a young child who has not yet been made aware of death. The child too may find such supportive third-party help invaluable for coping with the loss.

Never underestimate a child's grief or reaction to the death of a pet, as it can affect them in many different ways that can have long-lasting and detrimental effects on their behaviour, health, learning ability and socialization. One thing it is advisable not to do is to say that the pet was 'put to sleep', as this can create the false hope that one day their pet friend will wake up and come back again.

Pet grief

It is not just the owner who grieves over the loss of a pet: so can other animals in the household. The best thing to do is to carry on with the remaining pets' routine as normal, and to let them work out a new hierarchy among themselves.

Index

Acknowledgements

Special thanks

Hamlyn editors Trevor Davies, Clare Churly and Alison Copland; Stuart Davis; James Davis; Rosie Davis; Beryl Eddleston (retired Colourpoint Persian and British Blue breeder); Jen Lacey (Korat breeder); Chuck Cunningham (Mandala Exotic Cats/Chausies); Dr Paolo Pellegatta (Club Amatori Del Gatto Di Ceylon/Club of the Ceylon Cat Lovers); Jay Davis (Kremlin Cats/Peterbald); Lynne Couvier/Russian Hairless cats); Blake Gipson (Bemisu Cattery/Peterbald); Olga Anatova (Shining Beauty Cattery/Don Sphinx); Ingeborg Ekstrand (Yamsee Cattery/European Shorthair & Manx); Kristina Zimmermann (European Shorthair); Jaraslav Natski (Siberia Frost Cattery/Kurilean Bobtail); Barbara Long (USA Pride Cattery/Kurilean Bobtail); Svetlana Ponomavers (Kurilian Bobtail); Anthony Nichols (Quincunx LaPerms); Andy Lawrence (LaPerm); Beth Fillman (CalicoRose Cattery/Skookum); Dru Desy; Julia May (Oriental Shorthairs); Terri Harris (Munchkin); Naomi Johnson (Asian Group Cat Society); Tony Batchelor (German Rex); Kordula Möhle and Ilona Jaenicke (German Rex); The Ragdoll Fanciers' Club International; Susanna Toldi Bugge; Beth Gardner and Sue Manley (American Ringtail); Jo Parker; New Zealand Cat Fancy; Val Lewis; Dr Mirjam Kessler; Holly Webber (Foothill Felines/Bengals & Savannah); Patrick Kelley (Better Than Wild Cattery/Savannah); Gerald Zwiauer (Kanaani); Singapura Cat Club; Somali Cat Club (UK); Anke Baks (Cattery Yeni Raki/Anatolian); Steve Lloyd (Turkish Cat Society); Marianne Upham (Yenicizgi Turkish Van Cattery/Turkish Vankedisi); Turkish Van Cat Association; Anette Cederquist (Cederquist Cattery/Sokoke); Helle Lauridsen and Catherine Hidalgo (Sokoke); Susan Karakash (The KarakashKats Cattery/Serengeti); Sandra Roberts (City of Gold Cattery/Serengeti, bred by Allison Nevarro); Gary Fulgham (Safari Cat); Bion Kirk (Safari); Joe Childers (Timberline Cats/Highland Lynx); Bonni Huntoon (Highland Lynx); Linda Farrell (Rising Star Lynx/Desert Lynx); Lindsey D. Love (Desert Lynx); Jean Mill and Judy Sugden (EEYAA Cats/Toygers & Bengals); Fulvio Bresciani/International York Chocolate Federation); Allen Prichard; Arlene Magrino (The International Desert Lynx Cat Association); Linda Wright (Aloeway American Bobtails); Jacque Brown (The America Keuda Cat Association); Cora Cobb (Nebelheim Cattery/Nebelungs); Linna Ritch (Pixie-Bob); Anita H. Engebakken (Kimburu Cattery/Sokoke); Dr. Truda Straede (Chu Nintu Nestor Justinus Nestor, owned and bred by Dr. Straede, Founder of the Australian Mist Breed)

Many thanks to Rebecca Stevenson, MA VetMB MRCVS, Veterinary Technical Manager at Merial Animal Health, for her help with the Health section.

And thanks also to Chloe and Kira for their feline input on the Behaviour section.

Picture acknowledgements

Ardea/Frederic Rolland 151; /Jean-Michel Labat 104; /John Daniels 46 bottom right, 61, 74, 107, 162, 182 bottom left

Beth Fillman 121

Bonita Huntoon 123

Chanan Photography/Richard Chanan 77, 106, 124

Bruce Coleman Collection 112

Jason Couvier 127

John Daniels 183, 195, 196

DK Images 76, 79, 83, 98, 100, 100, 101, 102, 105, 115, 119

Helmi Flick Cat Photography 75, 82, 87, 113, 114, 117, 118, 120

Octopus Publishing Group Limited/ 9, 45 top, 45 bottom, 47 top, 47 centre, 47 bottom right, 47 bottom left, 49 top, 50, 65, 139, 143, 155, 170, 177, 189, 193; /Jane Burton 19, 21, 24 top, 26, 132 top, 141, 144, 145, 147, 167, 169, 173 top right, 175, 185, 187; /John Daniels 1, 12, 13, 15, 17, 18, 27, 29, 31, 34, 35, 37, 38, 39, 40, 130, 131, 132 bottom, 135, 136, 140, 142, 150, 153, 156, 157, 163, 165, 166, 179, 182 bottom right, 197, 201; /Nick Goodall 134; /Peter Loughran 7, 14, 52; /Ray Moller 22, 42-43, 44, 49 bottom, 51 bottom, 56, 57, 58, 59, 60, 62, 63, 66, 67, 68, 70, 72, 73, 81, 84, 92, 94, 95, 96, 97, 97, 99, 99, 102, 103, 108, 109, 125; /Steve Gorton 10, 11, 16, 20, 23, 32, 148, 159, 160, 164, 172, 173 top left, 199

Jacque Brown 91

Juniors Tierbildarchiv 80, 110

Bion Kirk 89

Lindsey D. Love 122

Nature Picture Library/Ulrike Schanz 71, 88, 93

Olga Antonova 126

The Picture Desk Limited/Art Archive 154

Sandra Roberts/City of Gold Cattery/Jim Childs 85

Bob Schwartz 86

Judy Sugden 90

Svetlana Ponomareva 116

Dr T M Straede 78

Warren Photographic/Jane Burton 8, 41, 46 top left, 64, 111, 184, 190

Acknowledgements

Acknowledgements

Executive Editor Trevor Davies
Editor Charlotte Wilson
Executive Art Editor Leigh Jones
Designer Peter Gerrish
Production Manager Ian Paton
Picture Researcher Vickie Walters